To, Andy P

13

PLYMOUTH ARGYLE
On This Day

PLYMOUTH ARGYLE
On This Day

History, Facts & Figures
from Every Day of the Year

RICK COWDERY

PLYMOUTH ARGYLE
On This Day

History, Facts & Figures from Every Day of the Year

All statistics, facts and figures are correct as of 1st September 2008

© Rick Cowdery

Rick Cowdery has asserted his rights in accordance with the Copyright, Designs and Patents Act 1988 to be identified as the author of this work.

Published By:
Pitch Publishing (Brighton) Ltd
A2 Yeoman Gate
Yeoman Way
Durrington
BN13 3QZ

Email: info@pitchpublishing.co.uk
Web: www.pitchpublishing.co.uk

First published 2008

A catalogue record for this book is available from the British Library.

10-digit ISBN: 1-9054113-0-8
13-digit ISBN: 978-1-9054113-0-6

Printed and bound in Great Britain by Cromwell Press

TO THE SEEKERS AND DREAMERS:
"LANG MAY YOUR LUM REEK"

Rick Cowdery – September 2008

ACKNOWLEDGEMENTS

Thanks to the peerless Mike Curno and to John Ashton, Alec Henderson, and all other keepers of Argyle records whose own labours of love have been invaluable reference sources, notably: WS Tonkin's All About Argyle; Brian Knight's Plymouth Argyle: A Complete Record 1903-1989; Terry Guswell and Chris Robinson's The Argyle Book; John Lloyd's Plymouth Argyle Football Club Classic Matches; Andy Riddle's Plymouth Argyle 101 Golden Greats and Plymouth Argyle: The Modern Era; Harley Lawer's Argyle Classics; and Steve Dean's Greens on Screen website. Thanks, too, to Dave Rowntree, for his photographs.

Rick Cowdery – September 2008

FOREWORD BY SEAN McCARTHY

I've been fortunate enough to be able to say that I've played my own small part in the history of Plymouth Argyle.

I've been a bit of a hero (Everton 1989) and a bit of a villain – leaving for Bradford in 1991; a hero, again – St James' Park 2000; and a pantomime villain, getting sent off (just before the Cheltenham Festival, coincidentally) on my return with Exeter in 2002.

I've been privileged to have played with the likes of Tommy Tynan and Kevin Hodges, John Uzzell and Kevin Summerfield; and to have played under Ken Brown and David Kemp, Kevin Hodges and Paul Sturrock. You can read about them and hundreds of other proud Pilgrims in the pages that follow.

I've played for more than a few clubs, in all divisions, and against many others and I can honestly say that Plymouth Argyle is unique and holds a special place in my heart. Don't ask me why – it just gets me that way. You know what I'm talking about, don't you?

After 176 games for Argyle between 1988-2001, and having settled in the Wescountry since hanging up my boots, I thought I knew a little bit about the Pilgrims. And I do, I know a little. Reading this made me realise just how little. I've known Rick Cowdery ever since I've been associated with the club and I can't believe he had kept so many things from me. You should be grateful he's decided to share them with you.

Sean McCarthy, Plymouth Argyle 1988-90, 1998-2001
176 games. 47 goals. Forever Green.

INTRODUCTION

A lot of water's flowed under the bridge, to borrow a favourite phrase of one of the 29 occupants of the Argyle manager's chair, since Frank Grose and William Pethybridge met in the Borough Arms coffee house – a century before anyone had heard of Starbucks – to discuss forming a football team.

If you have read the above paragraph and are thinking: "29? He's not counting the short-lived, quickly-abandoned, Neil Dougall-George Taylor joint-management experiment, nor any of the eight caretakers including Kevin Summerfield, who was in temporary charge twice", or if the mention of what the global village recognises as the self-styled "premier purveyor of the finest coffee in the world" brings to mind an Argyle midfielder of the late 1990s who made just six starts, then you'll enjoy this book.

Yes, it's a daily diary – bite-sized nuggets of easily digested information served up to satisfy the most voracious of any Janner's appetite… so eat up your Greens, with relish. However, it is also a journey… no, silly me… a Pilgrimage, from January to December; from Adams (George) to Wyllie – stop sniggering at the back; from Bedford Street to Obertraun, by way of Mount Gould, Marsh Mills, Devonport and Home, sweet home, Park.

It's also a drama, with an evolving cast of characters that no Pulitzer prize-winning playwright would dream of conjuring up: if Dave Smith did not exist, who would have dared to invent him? 'The Ciderman' features in the following pages, of course, alongside 'Jumbo Jack', 'Cocko', 'Ginger', 'Luggy', 'Miffy', 'Crudgie', and dozens and dozens of other Pilgrims who have played a part – sometimes big, sometimes small, but always significant – in the 120-plus years' history of English football's most westerly outpost.

It is a story, with a beginning but no end, of victories and defeats; of growth and stagnation; of hope and despair; of angels and sinners. Of dreams, often dashed, which survive through the combined spirit of the green-shirted heroes and those who have worshiped them through the ages. If you are still asking "is this the book for me?" put it down and go find the fiction section: you wouldn't understand the answer, anyway. For all true Pilgrims: enjoy.

Rick Cowdery – September 2008

PLYMOUTH ARGYLE
On This Day

P·A·F·C

JANUARY

MONDAY 1st JANUARY 1973

All-time great Michael Evans was born, in Plymouth. Evans made his debut in a Second Division game at Port Vale in 1990 and went on to appear 432 times for his hometown Greens before bowing out on the final day of the 2005/06 season on an emotional – and scoring – Home Park finale; a 2-1 Championship win against Ipswich. Only five men had pulled on the green shirt more times; Kevin Hodges, Sammy Black, Johnny Williams, Pat Jones and John Hore. Evans was also ninth in the list of all-time Argyle goalscorers on his retirement, with 80 goals.

WEDNESDAY 1st JANUARY 1986

The Pilgrims battled back from losing goalkeeper Geoff Crudgington, and going 4-2 behind to Cardiff City, at Home Park for a 4-4 draw that preserved a 13-game unbeaten Third Division home record. Full-back Gordon Nisbet took over between the posts with the score at 1-1 when Crudgington suffered a facial wound. Fifteen minutes into the second half, Nisbet had been beaten three times, with Kevin Summerfield's reply looking like mere consolation, but late goals from John Clayton and Kevin Hodges gained an unlikely point for Argyle.

MONDAY 2nd JANUARY 1995

Steve McCall was appointed Argyle manager in succession to Peter Shilton. His reign lasted 15 games – three wins, nine defeats – before he was replaced by former Ipswich team-mate Russell Osman, who he had brought in as a player. McCall will be better remembered as one of the greatest midfielders to ever play for the Pilgrims in two spells between 1992 and 2000. He was voted the fans' Player of the Year in 1993 and 1994 – one of only two Greens to receive the accolade in successive seasons.

WEDNESDAY 2nd JANUARY 2008

Barry Hayles made his loan deal to Leicester City permanent, rejoining his former Argyle manager Ian Holloway at the Walkers Stadium. Hayles had been leading goalscorer the previous season – his only full Pilgrims' campaign – with Argyle losing none of the 14 matches in which he scored.

SATURDAY 3RD JANUARY 1931

Argyle suffered a 6-3 home defeat by Bury in a struggling first season in the Second Division. In the same campaign, they also conceded seven at Bradford Park Avenue and nine at Everton. Remarkably, either side of the 9-1 defeat at Goodison Park, Argyle beat Cardiff City 5-1 at Home Park and won 4-0 at Barnsley.

SATURDAY 3RD JANUARY 2004

David Friio led the way as Argyle thrashed Chesterfield 7-0 on their way to the Second Division title. The French midfielder netted a hat-trick, scoring his first goal in the 15th minute when Argyle were already 3-0 up thanks to Lee Hodges, Tony Capaldi and Nathan Lowndes. Lowndes added another to bring up the fastest five opening goals scored in English League football. Friio completed his hat-trick in the final minute.

SATURDAY 4TH JANUARY 1936

Sammy Black scored all four goals as Argyle beat Port Vale 4-1 in a Second Division game at Home Park. The Scottish outside-left opened the scoring in the 15th minute before two goals in three minutes around the half-hour saw him complete his hat-trick. Vale pulled one back before the interval and a dull second half was brightened by a marvellous solo goal from Black.

SATURDAY 4TH JANUARY 1975

Billy Rafferty netted twice against his former club Blackpool as Argyle pulled off an FA Cup third round giant-killing, beating the Seasiders 2-0. Glaswegian Rafferty ended the season as the Pilgrims' leading goalscorer with 23 league strikes as Argyle won promotion to the Second Division.

SATURDAY 5TH JANUARY 1974

Red Devils superstar George Best went absent within hours of the kick-off of the FA Cup third round match between Argyle and First Division Manchester United at Old Trafford. Tony Waiters' Third Division Pilgrims also made an exit, going out of the competition to a headed second-half goal from Lou Macari. Best never played for United again.

FRIDAY 5TH JANUARY 1979

Bobby Saxton was appointed Argyle manager number 19. The former Pilgrims' half-back and captain returned to Home Park from Exeter City after Malcolm Allison ended his second term as Argyle chief by rejoining Manchester City. As a player, 'Sacko' made more than 250 appearances in seven years after joining the Pilgrims from Derby in 1968.

SATURDAY 5TH JANUARY 1980

Jeff Cook, on loan from Stoke City, and John Sims each scored twice as the Pilgrims humbled Hull 5-1 in a Third Division clash at Home Park. Cook, making his full debut, inspired the Pilgrims to a sixth successive win and began a scoring streak which saw him net in the following three games before he was recalled to the Potteries. The following year, he joined Argyle permanently and scored 21 goals in 55 games.

SATURDAY 6TH JANUARY 1951

For the second time in successive seasons, Argyle entertained First Division giants Wolves, captained by Billy Wright, in the third round of the FA Cup. The Third Division Pilgrims, hampered by an injury to Pat Jones who ended the game wearing a rugby skull-cup, went down 2-1. George Dews scored the Argyle goal.

SATURDAY 6TH JANUARY 1962

Second Division Argyle dumped a West Ham side managed by Ron Greenwood out of the FA Cup with a 3-0 victory at Home Park. Wilf Carter, Johnny Williams and Ken Maloy scored against a top-flight Hammers' 11 that included Bobby Moore, Geoff Hurst, Ken Brown – who later managed the Pilgrims – and Malcolm Musgrove, who also served on the Argyle management team.

SATURDAY 7TH JANUARY 1950

FA Cup-holders Wolves were held to a 1-1 draw at Home Park by an Argyle side that was relegated to the Third Division at the end of that season. The Pilgrims took the lead when outside-left Stan Williams beat namesake Bert – England's goalkeeper – but were taken to a replay by Sammy Smyth. Argyle lost the replay 3-0. More than 77,000 watched both games.

SATURDAY 7TH JANUARY 1984

Tommy Tynan's penalty in the third minute of injury-time earned Third Division Argyle a 2-2 FA Cup third round draw against Newport at Home Park, keeping them on the road to the semi-final. Ex-Newport striker Tynan beat former team-mate Mark Kendall to level the second of two goals from John Aldridge.

SATURDAY 8TH JANUARY 1949

A crowd of 40,000 saw Argyle giantkilled by Third Division Notts County, going out of the FA Cup 1-0 at Home Park at the third-round stage. Pilgrims' inside-forward Ernie Edds was made to rue missing an easy early chance as County, led by England striker Tommy Lawton, won, thanks to Jackie Sewell's goal.

SATURDAY 8TH JANUARY 1972

Former dockyard worker Derek Rickard upstaged debutant teenage keeper Peta Bala'c by grabbing a hat-trick in a 4-0 home Third Division win over York City. Referee Malcolm Sinclair needed two pre-match inspections to pass a greasy surface playable. Rickard, who had scored in the three previous games, claimed his hat-trick before half-time.

SATURDAY 9TH JANUARY 1932

There were no shocks at Home Park as Argyle eased past Manchester United 4-1 in the third round of the FA Cup. The Pilgrims, challenging for promotion from the Second Division, beat mid-table United through two-goal Tommy Grozier, Jack Vidler, and Jack Pullen.

SATURDAY 9TH JANUARY 1965

At 16 years and 323 days, Richard Reynolds was called up by Malcolm Allison to play in the Pilgrims' third round FA Cup tie against Derby at Home Park. The Looe forward helped Argyle to a 4-2 win, with Welsh international Barrie Jones scoring twice.

SATURDAY 10TH JANUARY 1953

Argyle reached the fourth round of the FA Cup for the first time in 16 years with a 4-1 home win over Coventry. The goals – from George Dews, Arthur Smith, Gordon Astall, and Alex Govan – came in the first half of a game which was the first at Home Park to feature a white ball.

TUESDAY 10TH JANUARY 1984

Andy Rogers scored the only goal of the game as Argyle won 1-0 against Newport in an FA Cup third round replay at Somerton Park. Despite only being in the third round, it was the Third Division Pilgrims' fifth FA Cup tie of the season – having already taken two games to dispose of Southend in the first round.

WEDNESDAY 11TH JANUARY 1950

Despite a midweek afternoon kick-off, a huge crowd of over 43,000 saw Argyle lose an FA Cup third-round replay 3-0 at Molineux, against First Division Wolverhampton Wanderers, with the home side including football icon and England skipper Billy Wright. Two goals in a minute, from Roy Swinbourne and a Johnny Hancocks' penalty, set Wolves on their way, with Sammy Smyth adding the third to put the result beyond any doubt. Argyle could console themselves with the very healthy gate receipts of more than £13,000 from the two cup games, including £8,000 from the first match – which was then a FA Cup record for any club in the third round of the competition.

SATURDAY 11TH JANUARY 1975

Argyle rose to second place in the Third Division, taking another stride to promotion, with a 7-3 thrashing of AFC Bournemouth at Dean Court. Paul Mariner, Billy Rafferty, Brian Johnson and Hugh McAuley scored in the first half, and Johnny Delve made it 5-0 straight after the break. The Cherries, aided by a Mike Green own goal, rallied to make it 5-3 before Mariner and Colin Randell restored the four-goal margin.

SATURDAY 11TH JANUARY 1964

Argyle drew 0-0 with Huddersfield Town in a Second Division game at Home Park, a week after being knocked out of the FA Cup third round, 1-0 by the same opponents, also in Devon. The two sides met an astonishing six times in the 1963/64 season in little more than four months – and Argyle did not win once. They lost 4-3 at Leeds Road in the league; drew 2-2 at Home Park in the first round of the League Cup; drew 3-3 in the replay at Leeds Road; and lost a second replay 2-1 at Villa Park.

SATURDAY 12TH JANUARY 1929

Sammy Black netted a hat-trick in a home FA Cup third round 3-0 victory over Blackpool as Third Division (South) Argyle overcame opponents from the league above them. Left-winger Black opened the scoring after six minutes and added his second 22 minutes later. The Scot completed his triple five minutes from the end of a comfortable win in front of more than 30,000.

MONDAY 12TH JANUARY 2004

Third Division title-winning defender Brian McGlinchey signed for Torquay United on a free transfer. Former Northern Ireland B international McGlinchey was manager Paul Sturrock's first permanent signing in 2000 and scored a memorable goal against Rushden & Diamonds early the following season that sparked a run which ended with the Third Division championship.

SATURDAY 13TH JANUARY 1906

Harry Wilcox scored a hat-trick against Sidcup College-based non-leaguers New Crusaders as Argyle won an FA Cup qualifying tie 6-3. It was New Crusaders' debut season and they went on to win the London Senior Cup Final before breaking away from the Football Association in 1907 to form the Amateur Football Association.

SATURDAY 13TH JANUARY 1934

A distinguished guest-list including Lord Mildmay of Flete Estate, the Lord Lieutenant of Devon, and the Earl and Countess of Edgcumbe saw Second Division Argyle hold Huddersfield 1-1 in an FA Cup third round tie at Plymouth. The gate of 44,526 is a Home Park record, although some sources suggest the figure is 43,426. The crowd was 8,000 more than the previous home best and the game broke all records for receipts – £3,205. Argyle lost the replay 6-2.

SATURDAY 14TH JANUARY 1967

Argyle broke Millwall's 59-match unbeaten home record when they went to The Den and won 2-1 in the Second Division – ending a barren streak which had seen them fail to win away for nine months. Goals from Mike Bickle and Alan Banks saw Argyle become the first side to leave The Den with two points for nearly three years.

TUESDAY 14TH JANUARY 2003

Argyle went out of the FA Cup to non-league opposition for only the second time in their history when they lost 2-0 in a third round replay at Dagenham & Redbridge. Goals from Ian Stonebridge and Paul Wotton in a 2-2 draw ten days earlier had earned the Second Division Pilgrims a second stab at the Daggers.

SATURDAY 15TH JANUARY 1927

Goalkeeper Fred Craig scored one of Argyle's goals in their 4-1 win over Third Division (South) promotion rivals Newport at Home Park. Craig, who played for the Pilgrims for 18 years, including their first ten seasons as a league club, netted Argyle's third from the penalty spot after fellow Scot Freddy Forbes had been brought down.

SUNDAY 15TH JANUARY 1978

Argyle defender Jon Beswetherick was born in Liverpool. 'Bezzie', a Home Park youth product, played 27 games at left-back during the club's record-breaking 2001/02 Third Division title triumph, having been more or less an ever-present in the previous two seasons. Medal in pocket, he left for Sheffield Wednesday after more than 150 games but found it difficult to replicate past glories.

SATURDAY 16TH JANUARY 1926

Jack Cock became only the second Argyle player to score four goals in a game, when the Pilgrims beat Norwich 6-3 in a Third Division match at Home Park. Cock ended the season with 31 league goals and surpassed that figure, by one, a season later to set a seasonal benchmark that has never been beaten.

SATURDAY 16TH JANUARY 1932

Jack Vidler hit a hat-trick as Argyle posted an 8-1 Second Division victory over Millwall, their biggest win at Home Park and their joint-biggest win anywhere. The first goal did not come until the 43rd minute, and the match entered its last half-hour with Argyle leading just 2-1, thanks to Vidler and Jack Leslie. However, six goals in 21 minutes declawed the Lions. Vidler bagged two more, Ray Bowden scored two, as did Sammy Black, and an own goal completed the rout.

MONDAY 16TH JANUARY 1961

Garry Nelson was born in Braintree, Essex. The left-winger-cum-striker joined the Pilgrims from Swindon in 1985 and was a key component of the Green Machine that was promoted to the Second Division in 1986. Such was his impact in his two years at Home Park – with 22 goals in 85 starts – that he was voted by fans into Argyle's Team of the Century.

SATURDAY 17TH JANUARY 1914

Fred Burch became only the second Argyle player since the club turned professional in 1903 to register a second hat-trick, which he achieved in a 4-1 Southern League away win against Bristol Rovers. Burch netted 95 goals in 245 league games.

SATURDAY 17TH JANUARY 1970

Argyle featured on television for the first time when they won 2-0 in a Third Division game at Luton Town. Mike Bickle and Derek Rickard scored in front of the *Match of the Day* cameras.

SATURDAY 18TH JANUARY 1992

Dwight Marshall hit a hat-trick in a 3-1 Second Division win at Barnsley, a rare highlight in a gloomy season for the Pilgrims, who were relegated at the end of the campaign – but stayed a Second Division side because of the league reorganisation following the establishment of the new Premier League.

FRIDAY 18TH JANUARY 2008

Steve MacLean became Argyle's first half-million pound signing when he joined the Pilgrims from Cardiff City. Scottish under-21 international MacLean began his career at Rangers and had a successful loan at Scunthorpe United, scoring 25 goals, before signing for Paul Sturrock at Sheffield Wednesday. He became the first Owl to score 20 goals in a season since Mark Bright, one of which was a crucial penalty in the League One Play-Off Final against Hartlepool United in 2005. Two injury-hampered campaigns later, he rejoined Cardiff City but, after recovering from ruptured ankle ligaments in a reserve game against Argyle, he was snapped up by Sturrock again.

TUESDAY 19TH JANUARY 1897

Bill Harper, who served Argyle as goalkeeper, trainer, groundsman and laundryman over a period of 50 years, was born. A Scottish international and Football League champion with Arsenal, his best playing days were behind him when he arrived at Home Park but he made more than 80 appearances before retiring. Such was his continuing influence until his death, aged 92, in 1989 that the Pilgrims' training ground is known as 'Harper's Park'.

WEDNESDAY 19TH JANUARY 1910

Argyle sustained their worst FA Cup defeat when they were hammered 7-1 by Tottenham Hotspur in a first round replay at White Hart Lane. Percy Humphreys led the way for Spurs with a hat-trick. Four days earlier, Spurs had been held to a 1-1 draw at Home Park.

SATURDAY 20TH JANUARY 1962

A crowd of 25,648 attended Argyle's reserve team fixture against Mansfield Town at Home Park. A week later, the Pilgrims entertained Double winners Tottenham Hotspur at the same venue.

WEDNESDAY 20TH JANUARY 1965

A weakened Argyle side pushed First Division Leicester City all the way before losing 3-2 in the first leg of the League Cup semi-final. Malcolm Allison was unable to select Barrie Jones, Nicky Jennings, Cliff Jackson and Frank Lord but Argyle twice took the lead, through Johnny Williams, with a trademark thunderbolt past England goalkeeper Gordon Banks, and, after Williams had put through his own net, when Mike Trebilcock followed up an incursion from debutant Glyn Nicholas. Bobby Roberts and Dave Gibson gave Leicester a lead to take to Home Park three weeks later.

SATURDAY 21ST JANUARY 1939

Inside-right Fred Mitcheson scored a hat-trick away when he netted three goals in 11 minutes to help the Pilgrims win a Second Division encounter 4-3 at Luton Town. The two teams went into the break with the Hatters winning 2-1, Dave Thomas having scored for the Greens. By the 56th minute, Argyle were 4-2 up with Mitcheson having dispatched two headers from crosses and a fine solo effort.

SATURDAY 21st JANUARY 1984

Two goals from Steve Cooper saw Argyle draw 2-2 with Lincoln City in a Third Division game at Home Park in which the Pilgrims played with ten men for all but the first three minutes, when Tommy Tynan was sent off for spitting at the Imps' Alan Walker, a player who later joined the Pilgrims for a two-game loan spell... after Tynan had left the club.

SATURDAY 22nd JANUARY 1927

A topsy-turvy game at Aberdare Athletic saw the Argyle go behind three times before edging a 6-5 win. On a snowy pitch, Alf Matthews and Jack Leslie equalised for the Pilgrims twice in the first half, but they still trailed 3-2 at the break. They turned it round with two goals apiece from Jack Cock and Sammy Black, but were given a nervous final five minutes when Aberdare scored.

SATURDAY 22nd JANUARY 1966

Mike Bickle netted a hat-trick as Argyle set their highest FA Cup score in beating non-league Corby Town 6-0 in the third round at Home Park. The Northamptonshire Southern Leaguers had knocked out Luton Town in the second round.

SATURDAY 23rd JANUARY 1915

The prolific Fred Burch netted this third hat-trick in less than two years when he scored all three goals in a 3-1 Southern League victory at Swindon Town.

WEDNESDAY 23rd JANUARY 1974

Having already knocked three First Division sides out of the League Cup, Argyle held top-flight Manchester City to a 1-1 draw in the first leg of the semi-final at Home Park. In front of a 30,000 Wednesday afternoon home crowd – the power crisis meant no floodlit games – Steve Davey took advantage of a slip by Willie Donachie to put Third Division Argyle ahead. City, though, called on the talents of Denis Law, Francis Lee, Colin Bell and Rodney Marsh to ensure that the second leg at Maine Road would start all square when Tommy Booth headed home a corner from Mike Summerbee.

SATURDAY 24TH JANUARY 1953

Inside-forward George Dews was forced unto an emergency role as goalkeeper when Argyle visited Rotherham United for a Second Division encounter, and, even though Dews conceded two goals in his 20-minute stint between the posts, the Pilgrims held on for a 3-2 win. Arthur Smith, in the first half, and Harold Dobbie and Alex Govan, in the second, put Argyle 3-0 ahead at Millmoor before goalkeeper Les Major injured his hand making a save and the Millers quickly nicked two goals.

SATURDAY 24TH JANUARY 1998

A goal from Simon Collins arrested a slide of five games without a win when Mick Jones' Second Division Pilgrims beat Wigan Athletic 3-2 at Home Park. Argyle had been winless since mid-December, when they had beaten Millwall 3-0 with Collins again on the scoresheet.

SATURDAY 25TH JANUARY 1936

More than 53,000 people packed into Stamford Bridge to see Argyle waste opportunity after opportunity in their FA Cup fourth round match against Chelsea, who took advantage of the Second Division Pilgrims' profligacy to win the tie 4-1.

SATURDAY 25TH JANUARY 1975

Welsh teenager Barrie Vassallo made a memorable debut when he scored Argyle's only goal in a 3-1 FA Cup fourth round defeat by Everton at Home Park in front of the *Match of the Day* cameras. Vassallo was called up by manager Tony Waiters to replace the injured Paul Mariner and briefly gave the Pilgrims hope of an upset when he reduced Everton's lead to 2-1 on the hour. However, the First Division side prevailed over their Third Division hosts thanks to Mick Lyons' later nerve-settler.

SATURDAY 26TH JANUARY 2002

The second part of the 2001-02 rebuild of Home Park was completed when the Lyndhurst Road stand re-opened for the Third Division game against Oxford United. Argyle celebrated in front of more than 8,000 fans with a 4-2 win in which Ian Stonebridge scored twice.

MONDAY 27TH JANUARY 1936

Argyle's 'other' John Williams was born. John Lloyd Williams, a regular in the Pilgrims' 1958/59 promotion season, was known as 'Cardiff' in recognition of his previous club, in order to avoid confusion with his same-name team-mate, also a half-back. His 15 minutes of fame came when he marked Jimmy Greaves in the Spurs man's first match back in England after leaving Italy.

SATURDAY 27TH JANUARY 1962

Double winners Tottenham Hotspur, led by Dave Mackay, proved too good for the Pilgrims as they eased into the fifth round of their defence of the FA Cup with a 5-1 win in front of just over 40,000 fans at Home Park. Jimmy Greaves scored twice.

SATURDAY 28TH JANUARY 1922

Frank Richardson scored three goals as Argyle overcame Brentford 4-1 in a Third Division game at Home Park. Richardson finished the season with 31 league goals – the joint-second highest tally by an Argyle player – including three hat-tricks in a five-month period.

SATURDAY 28TH JANUARY 1928

Norman Mackay scored a hat-trick on his debut as Argyle overcame Coventry 4-0 in a Third Division (South) match at Home Park. Mackay had joined from Scottish League Hearts and went on to make more than 240 league appearances for the Greens.

SATURDAY 28TH JANUARY 1933

First Vienna, Austria's oldest football club, visited Home Park for a friendly which ended 1-1. Vienna – whose right-back Karl Rainer had captained the Austrian national team against England and was one of 12 internationals in their squad – held the lead given to them by Siegfried Wortman until Eugene Melaniphy equalised five minutes from time.

SATURDAY 28TH JANUARY 1984

A late goal from Gordon Staniforth put Argyle into the last 16 of the FA Cup for the second time as the Pilgrims continued on the road to Villa Park with a 2-1 win over Darlington. Argyle had gone behind but came out for the second half level, thanks to a header from John Uzzell.

SATURDAY 28TH JANUARY 1989

Second Division Argyle came within 12 minutes of knocking an Everton side containing nine internationals out of the FA Cup but had to settle for a 1-1 fourth round draw. In front of the *Match of the Day* cameras, Sean McCarthy gave the Pilgrims the lead when he beat countryman Neville Southall in the Everton goal. An inexplicable handball by Pilgrims' defender Adrian Burrows allowed Kevin Sheedy to level from the penalty spot and take the tie back to Goodison Park, where Argyle lost 4-0.

SATURDAY 29TH JANUARY 1921

Goalkeeper Fred Craig, who scored five penalties in his Argyle career, made a late save to prevent Swansea Town from gaining an FA Cup second round draw in Wales. Craig defended Argyle's 2-1 lead, given to them by William Toms and Bertie Bowler, flinging himself full length to tip a free-kick away for a corner.

SATURDAY 29TH JANUARY 1927

Argyle's Third Division (South) game against Gillingham at Home Park ended in uproar when hundreds of fans surrounded Gills' goalkeeper James Ferguson after the game. Ferguson, who needed a police escort to reach the dressing-room, had enjoyed an outstanding game in the 0-0 draw – but he needed the local protection of local officers after he had wound up the home supporters during the match!

WEDNESDAY 30TH JANUARY 1974

Argyle's League Cup odyssey came to an end at Maine Road, where they lost 2-0 to Manchester City to go out of the competition one match from Wembley, 3-1 on aggregate. A goal early in each half from England midfielders Francis Lee and Colin Bell booked the eventual tournament winners a final place against Wolves.

TUESDAY 30TH JANUARY 2001

Ian Stonebridge scored twice as Argyle beat Kidderminster 4-0 at Home Park. Stonebridge was in the middle of a purple patch of seven goals in seven games. The former Tottenham Hotspur trainee was brought to Argyle by Kevin Hodges on a free transfer in July 1999, and scored 38 goals in 171 appearances.

SATURDAY 31st JANUARY 1931

Jack Vidler helped himself to a hat-trick as Argyle overcame West Bromwich Albion 5-1 in a Second Division match at Home Park. The pitch was waterlogged at kick-off and soon became a bog. Nevertheless, Vidler opened the scoring after half an hour and Sammy Black made it two before Ray Bowden took advantage of a ball that got stuck in the mud on its way to the Baggies' goalkeeper to give the Pilgrims a 3-0 interval lead. Two more from Vidler completed the drubbing.

THURSDAY 31st JANUARY 2008

Midfielder David Norris set a new Argyle transfer record when he moved to Ipswich Town for a reported £2.25m. 'Chuck' made 214 appearances for Argyle, scoring 26 goals, after being signed from Bolton for £25,000 in October 2002. He was an integral part of Argyle's promotion to the Championship in 2004, and was the fans' Player of the Year in 2005/06.

PLYMOUTH ARGYLE
On This Day

FEBRUARY

TUESDAY 1st FEBRUARY 1955

Jack Rowley was named Argyle player-manager, after having spent 18 years at Manchester United and with six England caps to his name. He prevented relegation to the Third Division in his first season, but could not perform the same trick in the subsequent campaign. His third season saw the Pilgrims flirt with having to apply for re-election to the Third Division (South). However, in 1958/59, he took Argyle to the championship of the first united Third Division. He was unable to build on that success, though, and tensions with the Board saw him resign with the club struggling in the Second Division.

THURSDAY 1st FEBRUARY 1968

Billy Bingham was appointed as the new manager of Argyle. Bingham had played at outside-right for Glentoran, Sunderland, Luton Town, Everton and Port Vale in a career that included 56 Northern Ireland caps. He had two spells as his country's national team manager, the first of which between 1967 and 1970 coincided with his appointment as Pilgrims' manager when the club was in the Third Division. After a fifth-place finish in his first season, disenchantment about the dual role grew as the Pilgrims' form – and league position – suffered.

SATURDAY 2nd FEBRUARY 1946

Argyle achieved their first victory since the end of the Second World War when Paddy Brown's hat-trick gave them a 3-2 home win over Wolverhampton Wanderers. The Pilgrims had been more badly affected by most by the hostilities and finished bottom of the first post-war competition, the Football League South. With Home Park badly hit by the blitz on the city, simply competing was a triumph.

SATURDAY 2nd FEBRUARY 1957

A memorable day for Neil Langman, as he scored a hat-trick in a 4-1 Third Division (South) game against Coventry City at Highfield Road. It was the third of his four hat-tricks, and came in the middle of the striker's best season for the club, with 18 goals in 34 league and cup games.

SATURDAY 3RD FEBRUARY 1923

Frank Richardson made FA Cup history when he scored all four goals in the Pilgrims' 4-1 victory over Bradford Park Avenue at Home Park, the most goals scored by one Argyle player in an FA Cup match and the first Plymouth hat-trick in the competition.

SATURDAY 3RD FEBRUARY 1940

After the abandonment of the football programme because of the Second World War, the league was split into ten regions. Argyle beat Bristol City 10-3 in a South West Regional League game, with Jackie Smith scoring four goals and Leonard Townsend hitting three. They won the league, not least of all because they could call on guest players stationed with the services in the Westcountry.

MONDAY 3RD FEBRUARY 1997

Neil Warnock's brief reign as Argyle manager came to an end when he was sacked by chairman Dan McCauley. Less than a year earlier, Warnock had led the Pilgrims to a Third Division play-off success against Darlington at Wembley, but the relationship between the two principles had begun to deteriorate even before then. Warnock was succeeded by his former assistant, Mick Jones.

SATURDAY 4TH FEBRUARY 1905

Argyle drew 1-1 at Newcastle United in the FA Cup first round, Bob Dalrymple scoring. Four days later, the two met back at Home Park and again shared two goals, with Jasper McLuckie on target for the Pilgrims. A second replay at Plumstead, London, five days later, was won 2-0 by the Magpies.

SATURDAY 4TH FEBRUARY 1933

Argyle overcame horrific injury problems at home to Swansea Town to gain a 1-0 Second Division win. The Pilgrims' problems began after Jack Vidler gave them a 54th minute lead. Almost immediately, centre-half Fred McKenzie had to be taken to hospital with a fractured leg. Later, Jimmy Rae was booted in the face and was led from the field with blood pouring from his nose and was later hospitalised with chest pains. McKenzie did not play again until the following season.

SATURDAY 5TH FEBRUARY 1927

Jack Cock scored the fourth and final hat-trick of his Argyle career in a 4-1 win at Watford. Cock was capped twice for England before he arrived at Home Park, debuting against Ireland in 1919 and scoring within 30 seconds, the third-fastest timed England goal of all time.

SATURDAY 5TH FEBRUARY 1955

Argyle were beaten 6-1 away at West Ham United in a Second Division game in 1955. The Pilgrims' goal was scored by Eric Davis, a local man who had come to the club from non-league Tavistock. Davis claimed 29 goals for Argyle between 1952 and 1957.

MONDAY 6TH FEBRUARY 1961

Argyle's League Cup fourth round replay against Aston Villa at Home Park might have gone unnoticed if it had not been for an unusual twice-taken penalty by Wilf Carter. Having seen Villa goalkeeper Nigel Sims save a kick which the referee ordered to be retaken, Carter rolled the ball forward a couple of yards for team-mate Johnny Newman to stride forward and crash home. The penalty, which Newman reprised with Mike Trebilcock three seasons later, gave the Pilgrims a 2-0 lead, but Villa ran out 5-3 winners, with Gerry Hitchens scoring a hat-trick.

TUESDAY 6TH FEBRUARY 1973

Argyle beat Scunthorpe United 3-0 in a Third Division game at Home Park. Steve Davey scored twice and Derek Rickard once in front of a crowd of 10,008, none of who realised that Rickard's goal came after he had already broken his leg.

SATURDAY 6TH FEBRUARY 1993

Kevin Nugent scored three goals as Argyle won 3-2 at home to Mansfield Town in the first season following the reorganisation of the leagues.

TUESDAY 6TH FEBRUARY 2007

Tony Capaldi became the most-capped Argyle international when he won his 21st Northern Ireland cap since joining the Pilgrims. Capaldi beat Moses Russell's 80-year-old record when he played in a 0-0 friendly against Wales at Windsor Park.

WEDNESDAY 7TH FEBRUARY 1906

Having held Aston Villa to a goalless draw at Home Park in the first round of the FA Cup, Southern League Argyle lost the replay against the holders and four-times winners 5-1.

SATURDAY 8TH FEBRUARY 1930

Moses Russell played the last of his 314 games for the Pilgrims in a 0-0 Third Division (South) draw at Gillingham. Prematurely bald because of childhood rheumatic fever, Russell was snaffled to Home Park from Merthyr Town, partly because most people believed him to be older than his 22 years. Once, at Luton Town, a fan was so incensed by Russell booting the ball out of play that he threw a stone at him. Russell ducked and the missile hit Pilgrims' goalkeeper Fred Craig.

SATURDAY 8TH FEBRUARY 1997

Mick Jones' first game in charge of the Pilgrims ended in a 2-2 Second Division draw at Luton Town. All the goals came in a 10-minute spell in the second half, with Argyle twice equalising through Adrian Littlejohn and Michael Evans, who had earlier missed a penalty after being fouled by future Home Park team-mate Sean Evers.

TUESDAY 9TH FEBRUARY 1943

Goalkeeper Pat Dunne, Argyle's Player of the Year in 1967/68, was born in Dublin. Dunne was the brother of Manchester United's European Cup-winning full-back Tony and had been with his sibling at Old Trafford where he was first-choice custodian, before falling behind Harry Gregg and Alex Stepney in the pecking order. Dunne joined the Pilgrims in February 1967. The following season, the Ireland international was unable to prevent Argyle being relegated to the Third Division but won the fans' admiration.

SATURDAY 9TH FEBRUARY 2008

A goal from Hungarian international Péter Halmosi gave Argyle a 1-0 Championship victory at Leicester City. The win was the Pilgrims' first in Leicester, at the 20th attempt, and all the more satisfying for coming against a side managed by Ian Holloway, who had suddenly decamped to the Walkers Stadium from Home Park the previous November.

WEDNESDAY 10TH FEBRUARY 1965

The Pilgrims bowed out of the League Cup at Home Park after losing the second leg of their semi-final 1-0 against top-flight Leicester City, who earned a 4-2 aggregate victory. Malcolm Allison's men succumbed to a goal from John Sjoberg, although they felt aggrieved about the award of the corner that led to the conclusive strike.

SATURDAY 10TH FEBRUARY 1990

John Gregory took temporary charge following the dismissal of Ken Brown, and saw his charges push promotion-chasing Sheffield United hard in a Second Division game at Bramall Lane before losing 1-0.

SATURDAY 11TH FEBRUARY 1956

Neil Langman scored a hat-trick as Argyle eased past Liverpool 4-0 in a Second Division game at Home Park. Langman, a local product from Bere Alston, didn't notch his first until the 51st minute. It was the last time that Argyle beat Liverpool.

SATURDAY 11TH FEBRUARY 1961

Argyle were ordered to close Home Park for two weeks following incidents that occurred in a 2-1 Second Division victory over Huddersfield Town. Although the Pilgrims won with goals from Jimmy McAnearney and Wilf Carter, referee Dennis Howell, the future Minister for Sport, was pelted with orange peel, paper cups and a beer bottle.

SATURDAY 12TH FEBRUARY 1927

Argyle beat Crystal Palace 7-1 in a Third Division (South) encounter, one of 11 times that the Pilgrims have scored seven against opponents at Home Park. Jack Leslie, who netted a hat-trick against Palace, played in six of those matches and scored at least one goal in each of them.

TUESDAY 12TH FEBRUARY 2008

Jamie Mackie made history as Argyle beat Barnsley 3-0 in a Championship match at Home Park, scoring the fastest debut goal ever for the Pilgrims. The former Exeter City striker took 11 seconds to net after coming on as a substitute, beating Tony Witter's previous best in 1992 by more than 50 seconds. Mackie scored a second goal later to add to Steve MacLean's opener.

SATURDAY 13TH FEBRUARY 1937

Despite leading 3-0 after half an hour, Argyle lost their Second Division encounter at Aston Villa when the home side staged two comebacks to win 5-4. The Pilgrims opened with a pair of Jacks – Vidler and Connor – scoring three times before two harsh penalty decisions. In the second half, Argyle, with Johnny McNeil a passenger, saw Frank Broome level but their hopes were revitalised when Jimmy Hunter gave them the lead. Villa equalised through Broome before Houghton completed his hat-trick.

SATURDAY 13TH FEBRUARY 1988

A marvellous solo goal from midfielder Kevin Summerfield gave the Pilgrims a 2-1 Second Division win over Ipswich Town at Portman Road. Summerfield ran from halfway and shrugged off a couple of challenges before selling last defender Frank Yallop a dummy and firing the ball past goalkeeper Jon Hallworth. Summerfield made more than 150 appearances for the Greens and later returned to serve the club as youth-team manager, caretaker-manager (twice) and Paul Sturrock's assistant-manager in the Scot's two occupancies.

SATURDAY 14TH FEBRUARY 1948

'Flash' Gordon Astall made his debut in a 3-1 Second Division defeat by Luton Town. Astall was an immensely strong man, as befitted a former Royal Marine. He was selected for England B while helping Argyle out of the Third Division (South) – the first Pilgrim to win England honours for three decades – and eventually moved to Birmingham City, where he joined former Home Park team-mate Alex Govan. The two played together for the Blues in the 1956 FA Cup Final and Astall won two England caps.

SATURDAY 14TH FEBRUARY 1953

Chasing an FA Cup quarter-final spot for the first time, Argyle were the victims of a Home Park giant-killing when they suffered a 1-0 home defeat to Third Division Gateshead. A division higher than their opponents and chasing promotion, the Pilgrims saw their dreams dashed by a goal from Ian Winter which continued a run that had accounted for Liverpool and Hull.

SATURDAY 15TH FEBRUARY 1947

It was a case of 2-3-4 for Argyle when they played Leicester City in a Second Division game at Home Park: the visitors contributed two own goals and fielded three goalkeepers as Argyle won 4-0. Foxes' goalkeeper Joe Calvert injured himself unsuccessfully trying to keep out an attempted clearance from his own defender Sep Smith. George Dewis took over and conceded the Pilgrims' second to Dave Thomas. Then Tom Eggleston tried his luck and let in two more: from Argyle's Lou Tinkler, and a shot which deflected off team-mate David Jones.

SATURDAY 15TH FEBRUARY 1958

Wilf Carter scored the third of his seven Argyle hat-tricks in a home 3-1 Third Division (South) victory over Queens Park Rangers. Only Sammy Black has scored more league goals for Argyle. Carter netted 134 times in 254 matches and was the club's leading scorer for six successive seasons from 1957 to 1963.

SATURDAY 16TH FEBRUARY 1946

Argyle goalkeeper Bill Shortt had a debut to forget in a Football League South game at West Ham United. Shortt, who went on to play more than another 350 first-team games for the Pilgrims, was beaten four times by Dan Travis, and three by Terry Woodgate, as Argyle lost 7-0.

SATURDAY 16TH FEBRUARY 1952

The Pilgrims lost 1-0 to Port Vale in a Third Division (South) game marred by snow and fog. The reporter who filed for the *Sunday Independent* summed it up thus: "Do not ask me what happened... I just couldn't tell you. In fact, I haven't the foggiest idea. I only know that Argyle lost 1-0. The players told me so when they came off."

FRIDAY 17TH FEBRUARY 1967

Rather than face a blank FA Cup weekend after being knocked out of the competition in the third round, Argyle hosted Dundee in a friendly and won 3-0. John Hore and Mike Bickle scored. The following month on fifth round Saturday, the Pilgrims beat Stoke City 2-1 in another friendly with goals from Johns Mitten and Newman.

SATURDAY 17TH FEBRUARY 2007

Argyle reached the quarter-finals of the FA Cup for the second time when they beat Championship rivals Derby County 2-0 in a fifth round tie at Home Park. Both goals were scored by on-loan forwards; Queens Park Rangers' Kevin Gallen and Scott Sinclair, who was on Chelsea's books at the time. Gallen netted from the penalty spot in the 14th minute, but had a second penalty saved by Derby keeper Steve Bywater, before Sinclair wrapped things up with a well-judged header five minutes from time.

SATURDAY 18TH FEBRUARY 1978

Argyle's home Third Division game against Bradford City was called off after an hour, with the visitors ahead 1-0, after referee Ron Crabb suffered from hypothermia. The Exeter prison officer called the game off because of icy winds when the back of his head went numb and he could not breathe properly. The official had unwillingly aided the Pilgrims' fight against relegation. Down to ten men after having Micky Horswill sent off, it is unlikely they would have scored six goals, as they did – without reply – when the game was re-staged.

SATURDAY 18TH FEBRUARY 1984

Argyle posted the most amazing FA Cup triumph in their history when they beat First Division West Bromwich Albion 1-0 in a fifth round tie at the Hawthorns. They belied their status as a struggling Third Division side to outplay their First Division opponents, led by new manager Johnny Giles. Striker Tommy Tynan scored the 58th-minute goal that booked the Pilgrims' place in the last eight of the competition.

SATURDAY 18TH FEBRUARY 2006

Vincent Péricard scored a hat-trick on his full home debut as Argyle beat Coventry City 3-1 in a Second Division game. The Cameroon-born former St Etienne and Juventus striker had been borrowed by manager Tony Pulis from his former club Portsmouth, and his Home Park bow was, by some way, the high point of his stay. He only scored one more goal for the club in a total of 15 games during his temporary stay in Devon.

SATURDAY 19TH FEBRUARY 1921

The Pilgrims nearly produced an FA Cup shock in their first season in the Football League when they took Chelsea to three games in the third round before the First Division side prevailed 2-1 in a second replay. The first game finished 0-0, with Chelsea's England striker Jack Cock, who would later go on to become one of Argyle's greatest strikers, being among those to draw a blank in front of a crowd of 27,749 that set a new Home Park record.

SATURDAY 19TH FEBRUARY 1983

Geoff Crudgington was twice a hero as Argyle beat Bradford City 3-1 in a Third Division encounter at Home Park. The Pilgrims' goalkeeper played despite second-degree burns to his midriff, the result of saving his home from a blaze earlier in the day when he flung a pan of burning fat out of his kitchen. With reserve-team 'keeper Neil Hands on his way to Devizes, full-back Gordon Nisbet was ready to take over between the posts before Crudgington opted to play through the pain. Mike McCartney's late penalty (against former Argyle goalkeeper Neil Ramsbottom) and Kevin Hodges' even later goal secured the win.

SATURDAY 20TH FEBRUARY 1960

Argyle suffered their heaviest defeat of the season when they went down 5-2 to Charlton Athletic in a Second Division game at the Valley. Ironically, Argyle's biggest win of the same campaign came against the same opposition, who the Pilgrims had hammered 6-4 at Home Park a few months earlier in October. Argyle's Wilf Carter scored in both games.

SATURDAY 20TH FEBRUARY 1982

A wonderful goal by Chesterfield's Alan Crawford was the highlight of an exciting Third Division match at Saltergate which ended level at 2-2. Crawford scored straight from the second-half kick-off when he ran from the centre-spot towards the Argyle goal, evaded a challenge from John Uzzell and planted the ball past Argyle goalkeeper and captain Geoff Crudgington. After receiving the ball, straight from the kick-off, no other player, team-mate or opponent, touched the ball before it hit the back of the net.

TUESDAY 21st FEBRUARY 1984

Argyle beat Torquay United 5-1 in the first round of the Associate Members Cup at Home Park. Future Gulls Tommy Tynan and Kevin Hodges scored two each in Argyle's debut in the short-lived competition. The Third Division Pilgrims went on to the last four, thus reaching two Cup semi-finals in the same season.

SATURDAY 22nd FEBRUARY 1997

Michael Evans and Mark Saunders steered Argyle to a 2-1 Second Division victory at Chesterfield in a game which saw five players sent off. Argyle held a goal lead going into the final minutes, having played for an hour without dismissed midfielder Ronnie Maugé, when Pilgrims' goalkeeper Bruce Grobbelaar was knocked out to spark a 20-man fight that saw two players from each side sent off: Argyle's Richard Logan and Tony James, and Chesterfield's Kevin Davies and Darren Carr.

TUESDAY 22nd FEBRUARY 2005

Argyle eased their Championship relegation worries with a 3-0 victory over Sheffield United at Home Park. Neil Warnock's side lost goalkeeper Paddy Kenny with a hip injury when they were already a goal down to Graham Coughlan's strike. With no substitute goalkeeper, Phil Jagielka took over between the posts and was beaten twice more, by Paul Wotton and on-loan Dexter Blackstock.

SATURDAY 23rd FEBRUARY 1957

Geoff Peach added his name to the list of footballers to have played just one Pilgrims league game when he lined up in a Third Division (South) match at Shrewsbury Town that Argyle lost 3-1. The Cornishman had played for the reserves as an amateur and established himself as a regular goalscorer.

SATURDAY 23rd FEBRUARY 1985

Mark Rowe played his last game for the Pilgrims in a 1-0 Third Division defeat at Bristol Rovers. The Cornishman represented Argyle 66 times after debuting as a teenager in 1981, but was the Pilgrims' unused substitute in the 1984 FA Cup semi-final. By the semi-final of the following year, Rowe had drifted into a long and successful non-league career.

SATURDAY 24TH FEBRUARY 1940

Leonard Townsend scored a hat-trick in a 4-1 win against Swindon Town at Home Park in the wartime South West Regional League. Townsend played for the Pilgrims seven times, scoring 10 goals.

SATURDAY 24TH FEBRUARY 1973

Spotland will always hold special memories for Argyle, not least of all for the 6-0 thrashing of Rochdale by Tony Waiters' side. The Pilgrims netted three goals in each half. Derek Rickard and Alan Welsh each scored two, with David Provan and Les Latcham also notching.

MONDAY 25TH FEBRUARY 1946

Argyle Player of the Year for 1976/77, Neil Ramsbottom, was born in Blackburn. It was Ramsbottom's only season at Home Park, between stints at Sheffield Wednesday and his home-town club, and Argyle were relegated to the Third Division. The custodian did enough to win the annual vote of the supporters before losing his place to Paul Barron.

SATURDAY 25TH FEBRUARY 1984

A crowd of 10,023 people watched Argyle win a Third Division game against Hull City 2-0 at Home Park, thanks to goals from Tommy Tynan and Dave Phillips... or did they? The figure was swelled as some people paid to get in twice to ensure that they had enough vouchers to claim a ticket for the Pilgrims' upcoming FA Cup quarter-final against Derby.

FRIDAY 26TH FEBRUARY 1932

Argyle forward Eric Davis was born, in Plymouth. The tall, slim, goalscorer joined the Pilgrims from Tavistock as a 20-year-old and made a scoring debut in a Second Division game away to Blackburn Rovers a year later. He scored 29 goals in 63 league games over four seasons before transferring to Scunthorpe, where he won the Third Division (North) championship.

TUESDAY 26TH FEBRUARY 2002

Marino Keith scored twice as Argyle won the last league derby against Exeter City 3-0 on their way to the Third Division title. In front of a 16,369 crowd, the Scottish striker fared better than former Pilgrim Sean McCarthy, who was red-carded for elbowing Graham Coughlan.

THURSDAY 27th FEBRUARY 1913

Perhaps the unluckiest Pilgrim, George Tepper, was born, in Doncaster. Given his debut in a Second Division game at home to Notts County towards the end of the 1933/34 season, he was hit in the eye by the ball and, as a result, never played league football again.

SATURDAY 27th FEBRUARY 1954

Neil Langman scored twice in his second game as Argyle hit four against Everton at Goodison Park… but still lost by four goals. Langman, 21, a part-timer still working for the South Western Electricity Board, started in place of the injured Maurice Tadman as Everton won the Second Division game 8-4. Langman went on to make 100 appearances for the Greens, many of them alongside his brother Peter. No Argyle game has seen more goals.

MONDAY 28th FEBRUARY 1921

After two goalless draws with the Londoners, Argyle finally succumbed to First Division Chelsea 2-1 in an FA Cup third round second replay at Bristol City's Ashton Gate. The Pilgrims were the first side to score after more than four hours of football when Williams Toms netted, but late Chelsea goals from Bob McNeil and Jimmy Croal settled the saga.

SATURDAY 28th FEBRUARY 1959

Jimmy Gauld scored a hat-trick in a 4-3 win at Swindon Town as Argyle fired their way to the Third Division title. By the following season the Aberdonian – who was later to become notorious as a match-fixer and served a four-year prison sentence for conspiracy to defraud – was playing for… Swindon.

SATURDAY 29th FEBRUARY 1992

With Peter Shilton waiting in the wings to become Argyle manager, caretaker duo Alan Gillett and Gordon Nisbet endured a miserable afternoon at Ipswich Town. Not only did the Greens lose their Second Division match 2-0, they also lost Robbie Turner to a broken leg after a collision with his own goalkeeper Rhys Wilmot. The match also marked the final game in the green for defender Andy Clement, after 42 league appearances.

PLYMOUTH ARGYLE
On This Day

MARCH

WEDNESDAY 1st MARCH 1961

Former player Neil Dougall was appointed Argyle manager following an unsuccessful spell in joint charge with another ex-Pilgrim, George Taylor: Dougall was named 'chief coach' and Taylor 'chief trainer' but the radical restructuring proved unworkable so, Dougall – who had played for the Pilgrims 289 times – was given sole responsibility for the first team and retained Taylor, who had made 48 appearances in the green, as his trainer. Eight months later, Ellis Stuttard was made manager, with Dougall moving back to chief coach.

SUNDAY 1st MARCH 1970

Ellis Stuttard was appointed Argyle manager for a second time, having previously filled the role between 1961 and 1953. A former Argyle player, he was chief scout to Billy Bingham when the Irishman left in 1970 and was asked to take the helm again. Two years later, he stood down to make way for Tony Waiters but remained at the club, filling various roles, and was honoured with a testimonial match against Nottingham Forest in 1979.

THURSDAY 1st MARCH 1990

March 1 seems to be a popular day for appointments at Home Park. The third Argyle manager to take up the cudgels on St David's Day was – appropriately enough – David Kemp, who, like his March 1st managerial predecessors, was another former Pilgrims' player. Kemp's managerial career began with Swedish side Norrköping before he was recruited to the Wimbledon coaching staff. Despite keeping Argyle competitive on a shoestring in the Second Division, he was blighted by his association with his previous employers, and, unfairly perceived as a 'long-ball' merchant, he lasted less than two years. He later came to Home Park for a third time, in his third different role, as assistant-manager to Tony Pulis.

SATURDAY 2nd MARCH 1935

Argyle beat Barnsley 4-1 in a Second Division game at Oakwell. The first of the quartet came from defender Harry Roberts, a penalty-specialist who relied on clout. This time was no different as he broke the Tykes' goalkeeper's fingers with the power of the shot.

MONDAY 2ND MARCH 1992

David Kemp's successor as manager was the biggest name to have played for the Pilgrims and much was expected of 125-times capped former England goalkeeper Peter Shilton when he was appointed by chairman Dan McCauley. Unfortunately, the tale of his management was also a tale of the deteriorating relationship between the two. Shilton took the side down from Division Two to the third tier at the end of his first part-season and, despite being given handsome financial backing, the side ended the following campaign in mid-table. The subsequent campaign was one of the best in the club's lower-league history but ended in play-off semi-final defeat to Burnley. Six months later, amid a very public and acrimonious stand-off between chairman and manager, Shilton was relieved of his duties.

SATURDAY 3RD MARCH 1990

David Kemp's first match in charge ended in a 3-0 Second Division Home Park victory over Sunderland, with Tommy Tynan scoring twice. The match also marked the first appearance in the green for former caretaker-manager John Gregory, two years after he last kicked a ball. Ex-England international Gregory, who had been brought to Home Park by former manager Ken Brown, played twice more before moving to Bolton Wanderers.

WEDNESDAY 4TH MARCH 1959

Argyle lost 4-2 at home to Accrington Stanley in a Third Division game. It is the only time that the Pilgrims have entertained the Owd Reds and one of only two home defeats they suffered in the 1958/59 season as they won the first combined Third Division title.

SATURDAY 4TH MARCH 1961

Wilf Carter scored a hat-trick as Argyle beat Leeds United 3-1 in a Second Division game at Home Park. Chairman Ron Blindell claimed credit for the victory, revealing afterwards that he, rather than his newly-appointed manager Neil Dougall, had made tactical changes at half-time. The fact that Leeds had two injured players as virtual passengers – including Jack Charlton – helped the comfortable Argyle win.

TUESDAY 4TH MARCH 2003

Argyle beat Peterborough United 6-1 in a Second Division game at Home Park. Posh had arrived in Plymouth having not conceded a goal away from home for ten weeks but found themselves 4-0 down at half-time as Marino Keith, David Friio, Paul Wotton, and a Sagi Burton own goal, put the game beyond United. Wotton's goal came in nine minutes of stoppage-time added on after Argyle centre-back Graham Coughlan had ripped the opposition's goal-netting following a rather too enthusiastic header. Second-half goals from Friio and Jason Bent completed the rout.

SATURDAY 5TH MARCH 1955

Luton Town goalkeeper Roy Baynham had an afternoon to forget when the Hatters visited Home Park for a Second Division game that Argyle won 2-1. Baynham took to the field with eight stitches in a head wound and gifted the Pilgrims their first when he mistakenly thought he had heard the referee's whistle and rolled the ball towards the edge of his penalty area, from where Eric Davis scored. Argyle went further ahead when the Town custodian – having given away a free-kick for 'carrying' – dropped Davis's shot over his goal-line.

TUESDAY 5TH MARCH 1991

Argyle drew 2-2 at West Ham United in a Second Division game in which future Argyle assistant-manager Tim Breacker played a huge part in denying the Pilgrims a victory. Breacker had a hand in the game's opening goal when his cross was turned into his own net by Pilgrim Nicky Marker. Two Robbie Turner headers turned the game the Greens' way before, with 12 minutes to go, right-back Breacker raided forward and equalised against his future employers.

SATURDAY 6TH MARCH 2004

Argyle drew 0-0 with Notts County in a Second Division game at Meadow Lane, in what was the first match after the resignation of manager Paul Sturrock. The Pilgrims' point was down, in large part, to goalkeeper Luke McCormick, who saved Paul Heffernan's penalty after Peter Gilbert had been harshly adjudged to have handled in the area.

SATURDAY 7TH MARCH 1959

Argyle players claimed eight goals in a game at Home Park for only the second time ever – although, technically, they actually only scored six in the 8-3 Third Division victory over hapless Mansfield Town. The other two came from Stags' defender Terry Swinscoe, who began and ended a bizarre afternoon. Argyle were 3-0 up after 20 minutes, with Alex Govan and Harry Penk having added to Swinscoe's first oggie, but, within half an hour, Mansfield were level. Argyle shot back through Jimmy Gauld and kicked for home with Johnny Williams bagging a brace and Wilf Carter scoring a penalty before Swinscoe added a second of his own. It remains the most goals ever scored in a Football League game at Home Park.

SATURDAY 7TH MARCH 1998

Argyle centre-back Richard Logan was dismissed in a Second Division game against Preston North End at Home Park. Despite being without Logan for the last 18 minutes of the match – he was sent off as he received a second yellow card – the Greens did well to hold onto a 2-0 lead, which had come courtesy of goals by Paul Wotton and Barry Conlon. A week later, Logan received another red, this time for a professional foul against Wycombe Wanderers at Adams Park. That dismissal proved much more costly: Argyle were trounced 5-1.

SATURDAY 8TH MARCH 1913

Fred Burch scored a hat-trick as Argyle overcame Merthyr Town 5-0 in a Southern League match at Home Park. Bertie Bowler and an own goal completed the scoring.

SATURDAY 8TH MARCH 1986

A Russell Coughlin penalty and a goal from Kevin Godfrey – his only strike in seven games on loan from Leyton Orient – gave the Pilgrims a 2-1 Third Division victory at Bristol Rovers to begin a club-record run of nine consecutive league wins. The run was brought to an end – after further victories at Wolves, Chesterfield, Bournemouth and Cardiff, and home wins over Walsall, Derby, Rotherham and Bury – 39 days later, when the Pilgrims were held 1-1 at Lincoln City.

SATURDAY 9TH MARCH 1940

Bill Archer hit a hat-trick as Argyle beat Newport County 3-0 at Home Park in the wartime South West Regional League. Archer did not find the target in 19 Football League games but got nine goals in the regional competition, after which he didn't play for the club again.

TUESDAY 9TH MARCH 1993

Argyle beat Blackpool 2-1 in a Second Division game at home despite the 19th minute sending-off of Jock Morrison. Hewn out of Aberdonian granite, popular centre-back Morrison was never far from controversy throughout his career. After post-Plymouth spells at Blackburn Rovers, Huddersfield Town and Blackpool, he became a fans' favourite at Manchester City, where he was famously sent off for sticking out his tongue at Stan Collymore, and cautioned by Merseyside police for squirting Liverpool fans with water.

WEDNESDAY 10TH MARCH 1909

Inside-left Tom Hakin earned a place for himself in Argyle folklore when he scored a hat-trick against local rivals Exeter City in a home Southern League game.

SUNDAY 10TH MARCH 1974

Argyle made Football League history when they finished 'Black Sunday' with only eight men in a 2-1 Third Division defeat at Port Vale. Goalscorer Steve Davey was sent off after 17 minutes, with Dave Provan and Bobby Saxton following late in the second half for clashing with Vale players in two separate instances. Argyle also had to contend with top striker Paul Mariner having his nose broken in their first Sunday Football League game.

SATURDAY 10TH MARCH 1984

Argyle's first FA Cup quarter-final ended in a goalless draw as Second Division Derby County escaped from Home Park to fight another day. They were kept in the game against their Third Division hosts by goalkeeper Steve Cherry, who went on to have two spells at Home Park. His notable save came late on when he tipped Gordon Staniforth's shot on to a post. The ball rebounded square and hit Cherry's other post before dropping on the goal-line.

SATURDAY 11TH MARCH 1939

On four separate occasions, Argyle have gone five straight league matches without scoring a goal – the club's equal worst run of matches without a goal. Coincidentally, two of those runs have started on March 11. Firstly, in 1939, when a 0-0 Second Division draw at home to Chesterfield preceded games at: Tranmere Rovers (a) 0-2; West Ham United (h) 0-0; Bury (a) 0-3; and Spurs (a) 0-1. Then again in 1950, March 11 signalled the start of five games without a goal. The Pilgrims, then also in the Second Division lost 2-0 at home to Queens Park Rangers, and followed that with games at: Preston North End (a) 0-0; Swansea Town (h) 0-1, Coventry City (a) 0-3; and Luton Town (h) 0-0. In 1938/39 it wasn't too much of a problem, as Argyle finished in mid-table of the Second Division, but in 1950 it had devastating consequences: the club were relegated to the Third Division.

SUNDAY 11TH MARCH 2007

Argyle's attempts to reach the semi-finals of the FA Cup for the second time were thwarted by the same team that had beaten them on the only occasion they made the last four. In front of the live *Match of the Day* cameras, the Pilgrims went out 1-0 at home to Watford – but with heads held high and their reputation enhanced – although ultimately there was no glory. After going behind to a 21st-minute goal from Hornets' Hameur Bouazza, following a sleepy start to their first FA Cup quarter-final for 23 years, the Pilgrims woke up. Wave after wave of pressure failed, though, to crack a Watford defence that, having been honed by weeks of Premiership poundings, somehow held firm. The crowd of 20,652 is the highest-ever at the rebuilt Home Park.

TUESDAY 11TH MARCH 2008

Argyle utility man Lee Hodges lived up to his billing when he took over in goal during the Pilgrims' 1-0 Championship defeat at Scunthorpe United. In donning the gloves after Luke McCormick was sent off for handling the ball outside the penalty area, Hodges completed the full set of playing positions for Argyle. He started off as a striker in a loan spell from Tottenham Hotspur, had begun matches in all the midfield and both full-back positions, and filled in at centre-back during injury-affected games.

SATURDAY 12th MARCH 1977

Kevin Smart, a product of the Argyle youth set-up, made his debut in a 1-1 Second Division draw at Luton Town to help deprive the home side of a tenth straight win. George Foster scored for the Pilgrims, with the Hatters' John Aston levelling. Smart went on to make another 31 league appearances for the Greens.

SATURDAY 12th MARCH 1988

Tommy Tynan scored the 200th league goal of his career in Argyle's 3-0 home Second Division win over Stoke City, and followed it immediately afterwards with his 201st. Tynan netted in the 32nd and 34th minutes, thanks largely to two assists from long-time team-mate John Uzzell, who marked his return to the starting XI after a long absence with the third.

WEDNESDAY 13th MARCH 1991

There was a comedy of errors at the Hawthorns. Not on the pitch, where Argyle came from behind to win their Second Division match against West Bromwich Albion 2-1. The Pilgrims went a goal down – although Carlton Palmer's strike did not look as if it had crossed the goal-line – but they bounced back with goals from Kevin Hodges and Robbie Turner. The cock-up came when Argyle introduced two substitutes, Mark Damerell and Jock Morrison, and both wore the number 14 shirt!

WEDNESDAY 14th MARCH 1973

Mike Dowling never scored in the league in his short career for Argyle – yet he will always be remembered for one of Home Park's iconic goals: a fantastic opener in a 3-2 friendly victory over Pele's Brazilian club side Santos in front of a crowd of 37,639. When Santos officials saw the crowd-size at the latest game on their world tour, they demanded a payment on top of what had already been agreed. No pay, no play. Pilgrims' chairman Robert Daniel was over a barrel, so he agreed to the ransom demand – but Argyle got their own back on the pitch! Dowling opened the scoring and Derek Rickard and Jimmy Hinch made it 3-0 at the interval. After the break a penalty from the world's greatest player Pele and a goal from Edu made the scoreline respectable.

WEDNESDAY 14TH MARCH 1984

Andy Rogers' winner, direct from a corner, gave Argyle a 1-0 FA Cup quarter-final replay win over Derby County at the Baseball Ground to take them into the last four of the competition for the only time. The fluke goal came in the 17th minute, from the Pilgrims' first corner of the game, which swung in over the head of goalkeeper Steve Cherry.

TUESDAY 15TH MARCH 1994

Argyle beat Rotherham United 3-0 at Millmoor to go top of the Second Division. They had to made work hard for the spoils, with Kevin Nugent breaking the deadlock in the 76th minute. Michael Evans hit a second almost immediately, and added a late third.

SATURDAY 15TH MARCH 2008

After 21 consecutive games without a win at Ashton Gate stretching back 77 years, Argyle beat Championship leaders Bristol City 2-1. Two goals from Rory Fallon put the Pilgrims ahead before a penalty from City substitute Lee Trundle. The game was also notable for the first appearance for 15 months of Pilgrims' captain Paul Wotton, after a knee injury, and a first appearance ever for goalkeeper Rab Douglas, who had been borrowed from Leicester City for one match to replace suspended Luke McCormick. Douglas began and ended his Argyle career without ever entering Plymouth.

SATURDAY 16TH MARCH 1946

Argyle survived a battering from Birmingham City to register a shock Football League South 1-0 win at St Andrews. Paddy Brown's headed winner four minutes from time for bottom-of-the-table Argyle proved to be the ultimate coupon-buster against league leaders and FA Cup semi-finalists City as the Pilgrims chalked up their first away victory of the season.

THURSDAY 16TH MARCH 1978

Malcolm Allison was appointed Argyle manager for the second time. Just like the first time, 14 seasons previously, he stayed for one year, and, just like 14 seasons earlier, he left for Manchester City. The Pilgrims finished 15th in the Third Division in his second spell.

SATURDAY 17TH MARCH 1906

Argyle beat New Brompton 5-0 in a Southern League fixture at Home Park, thanks to goals from Percy Saul, Tommy Briercliffe, Harry Wilcox (2), and Freddie Buck. The Pilgrims played New Brompton 18 times and lost only once, until New Brompton adopted a new name – Gillingham.

SATURDAY 17TH MARCH 1928

Percy Richards claimed a Third Division (South) hat-trick in just ten minutes against local rivals Torquay United, as the Pilgrims won 4-1 at Home Park. Richards netted ten times in 18 games during this, his first season, but found it hard to displace Ray Bowden from the team and joined Tunbridge Wells in 1931.

SATURDAY 18TH MARCH 1961

Argyle lost 2-1 to Ipswich Town in a Second Division match which was played at home… at Plainmoor. The Pilgrims had been forced to play at the home of their Devon neighbours after the Football Association closed Home Park for a fortnight following crowd disorder. Only 9,626 watched the game, which had, at one point, been scheduled for Tottenham Hotspur's White Hart Lane ground.

SATURDAY 18TH MARCH 1978

Malcolm Allison inspired Argyle to a first home win in Division Three for more than four months, two days after taking over for his second spell at Home Park. A late goal by Brian Johnson began a recovery that saw the Pilgrims avoid relegation by losing just three of their 12 matches of the season under Allison, who had replaced Mike Kelly.

SATURDAY 19TH MARCH 1921

Argyle defender Septimus Atterbury was sent off in a 1-1 Division Three (South) draw at Luton Town. The left-back walked after taking revenge on the Hatters player who fouled Pilgrim Jimmy Dickinson. Atterbury played only 30 times for Argyle in the Football League – all in their first season – but had been with the club for 13 years in the Southern League and stayed on at Home Park, as part of the coaching team, after his playing days.

FRIDAY 19TH MARCH 1926

Ernie Edds, who enjoyed two spells at Home Park, was born in
Portsmouth. Edds was signed from the Army after the Second
World War and scored 14 goals in 23 appearances, including a
hat-trick in a 3-2 Second Division victory over Southampton at
the Dell in the 1947/48 season. He later returned to Argyle from
Torquay United for another 26 league games, and four goals.

SATURDAY 20TH MARCH 1982

Argyle beat Walsall 4-1 in a Third Division game at Home Park.
The visitors finished the match with nine men after captain Brian
Caswell was sent off for abusive language and Mark Rees was
dismissed for two bookable offences. The Saddlers lost their heads
when team-mate Ken Beech was carried off following a Chris
Harrison tackle. Jeff Cook scored twice.

SATURDAY 21ST MARCH 1970

Derek Rickard scored a hat-trick as Argyle beat Shrewsbury Town
4-2 in a Third Division game at Home Park. It was Plymothian
Rickard's 17th game after leaving his dockyard job to turn
professional and he already had five goals under his belt.

TUESDAY 21ST MARCH 1978

Malcolm Allison's first away game in his second spell as Argyle
manager ended in a 5-1 Third Division victory at Portsmouth.
Teenage substitute Mike Trusson returned after five months out
injured to give Argyle a lead in the Battle of the Ports, which Fred
Binney doubled before half-time. Brian Taylor scored a free-kick
before Keith Fear added a fourth. Binney completed the crushing.

SATURDAY 22ND MARCH 1924

Jack Smith netted a Home Park hat-trick in Argyle's 4-0 Division
Three (South) game against Bournemouth & Boscombe Athletic.
Percy Cherrett claimed the other. The fixture list that season had a
strange look to it with, largely, Argyle playing the same opposition
on two consecutive weekends, alternatively at home and away. Thus,
the week prior to Smith's triple, the Pilgrims had drawn 0-0 at their
south-coast rivals.

SATURDAY 22ND MARCH 1969

Having just been crowned League Cup winners, Swindon Town were brought down to earth with a bump when Argyle beat them 2-1 in a Third Division game at Home Park, just a week after the Robins' shock Wembley victory over First Division Arsenal. Two goals from Mike Bickle saw the Pilgrims come out on top of a match which was a triumph for the tactics of Argyle manager Billy Bingham that kept winger Don Rogers – the man who had shot down the Gunners at the Twin Towers – quiet.

SATURDAY 23RD MARCH 1963

Three days after his debut, Pilgrims' teenager Richard Davis went head-to-head with one of English football's greatest-ever players, 48-year-old Stanley Matthews, as Argyle lost 1-0 in a home Second Division game against Stoke City. Plymothian Davis was one of two 19-year-old full-backs, along with Dave Roberts, charged with keeping quiet a Stoke forward line that also included Jackie Mudie, Dennis Viollet and Jimmy McIlroy. It was Sir Stan's only official Home Park visit, although he had played for Blackpool in a floodlit friendly nine years earlier.

SATURDAY 23RD MARCH 1968

Colin Sullivan, aged 16 years and 269 days, made his bow in a Second Division victory over Millwall at Home Park, the third-youngest Pilgrim debutant. Sullivan was handed his start by Billy Bingham in a game won 2-1 thanks to two Norman Piper goals. Sullivan played another 255 times for the Pilgrims and was voted the club's best-ever left-back when the Team of the Century was chosen in 2004.

SATURDAY 24TH MARCH 1934

Forward Len Featherby endured a miserable spell at Argyle, playing just eight games across two seasons, including a 3-2 Second Division defeat at Fulham in which he was injured. It was Featherby's second appearance for the Greens, having joined eight days earlier from Merthyr Town. He was one of three players badly hurt at Craven Cottage – where Jimmy Cookson and George Briggs scored – and barely played again.

SATURDAY 24TH MARCH 1984

Not a day to be a Smith, as the Pilgrims went down 5-0 to eventual Third Division champions Oxford United at the Manor Ground. Mark Smith, making the first of his three appearances for the Pilgrims, conceded a penalty which Bobby McDonald converted; Steve Biggins netted a 22-minute hat-trick; then Lindsay Smith conceded another penalty for McDonald to complete the home side's nap hand.

SATURDAY 25TH MARCH 1972

Argyle drew 0-0 at home to Port Vale in a Third Division stalemate at Home Park in which not only the supporters were moaning. Pilgrims' midfield Les Latcham called the encounter "the worst game I have ever played in" while manager Ellis Stuttard reacted to the opposition's 10-man defence by saying: "Their tactics would have floored Real Madrid."

SATURDAY 25TH MARCH 2000

Paul McGregor scored the first Argyle hat-trick of the 21st century with a Third Division treble in a 4-0 win against Torquay United at Plainmoor. The third goal was stroked through the Gulls' keeper's parted legs and the accompanying yell of 'nuts' ensured the diminutive striker came in for some special attention when the two teams clashed the following season.

SATURDAY 26TH MARCH 1988

Ossie Ardiles – brought in by Blackburn Rovers to aid their push for promotion to the top-flight – had a miserable debut at Home Park as Argyle won 3-0, with goals from Stewart Evans, Adrian Burrows and Kevin Hodges. Ardiles limped from the field after just 50 minutes, the victim of a robust challenge from future Blackburn player Nick Marker.

TUESDAY 26TH MARCH 2002

Argyle beat Rochdale 3-1 at Spotland to win promotion to the Second Division. Strikes from Marino Keith, Graham Coughlan, and Lee Hodges guaranteed that Paul Sturrock's Pilgrims moved up a division with six matches to spare. Sturrock became only the second Argyle manager to win promotion in his first full season, after Neil Warnock. The defeat was Rochdale's second of the season at home.

SATURDAY 27TH MARCH 1954

Neil Langman scored his first hat-trick in league football five weeks after turning professional as Argyle won a Second Division encounter against Derby County at the Baseball Ground, 4-1. Langman's introduction to the Pilgrims' fight against relegation was the key to them surviving the drop as he scored nine goals in just nine matches.

SATURDAY 27TH MARCH 2004

Argyle drew 0-0 at home to Wrexham in a Second Division game despite the Welsh side finishing with nine men after Craig Morgan and Darren Ferguson were dismissed. Before the game, 100 former players took part in the 'Parade of Pilgrims', part of the club's Centenary Year celebrations. Star turn was Marcus Montagu Murphy, who, despite being 89, could not resist one last sprint down the touchline.

MONDAY 28TH MARCH 1932

Argyle beat Oldham Athletic 5-0 in an Easter Monday Second Division clash at Home Park, having won the reverse fixture 3-1 on Good Friday. The Pilgrims managed to slip up on a trip to Wolves on the Saturday in between, which they lost 2-0. They bounced back on the Monday thanks to two goals each from Jack Leslie and Eugene Melaniphy, and another from Harry Roberts.

SATURDAY 28TH MARCH 1987

Argyle lost 4-0 to FA Cup semi-finalists Leeds United in a Second Division fixture at Elland Road, where future Pilgrim Ian Baird scored a hat-trick to ruin Stewart Evans' debut. Baird also had a hand in the first, winning a penalty that Gordon Strachan converted.

SATURDAY 29TH MARCH 1913

Fred Burch scored four goals in a 6-1 Southern League home win over Southampton. The game was the first of six straight wins – in which Burch scored another six to ensure that the Pilgrims won the title.

FRIDAY 29TH MARCH 1929

Just over a year after scoring a Third Division (South) Home Park hat-trick against Torquay, Percy Richards scored a Third Division (South) Home Park hat-trick against Torquay United.

FRIDAY 30TH MARCH 1923

Jack Fowler made it a very Good Friday when he scored a hat-trick in a 5-1 Third Division (South) derby victory against Exeter City at Home Park, the first triple in league matches between the sides.

TUESDAY 30TH MARCH 1999

Steve Guinan made an instant impact on his home debut following his loan move from Nottingham Forest, scoring a hat-trick in a 5-0 thrashing of Scunthorpe United. Guinan scored seven goals in 11 matches but later signed a permanent deal with Cambridge United. He left the U's three months later and returned to Home Park, and scored three goals in 19 starts before being released by Paul Sturrock.

TUESDAY 31ST MARCH 1959

John Uzzell, who made 340 appearances across 12 seasons with his home-town club, was born. Defender Uzzell made his debut as 18-year-old on the opening day of the 1977/78 Third Division season and held his place for the rest of the campaign. He was not a regular again until 1981, staying put for three seasons, and was a member of the 1984 FA Cup semi-final team. After that, he was again a fiddler's elbow of a choice before moving to Torquay United, where his career was brought to a premature end after a horrific injury sustained in a clash with Brentford's Gary Blissett.

WEDNESDAY 31ST MARCH 2004

Defender Tony Capaldi became the first Pilgrim for 20 years to win a full international cap for one of the home nations. The Norwegian-born Brummie represented Northern Ireland against Wales, taking on a baton passed to him by German-born Welshman Dave Phillips.

SATURDAY 31ST MARCH 2007

Mathias Kouo-Doumbe was controversially red-carded after a mere 83 seconds of Argyle's 3-0 Championship defeat at Ipswich Town – the quickest-ever sending off in Pilgrims' history. "There was small contact between us, but nothing special," said the centre-back of his clash with Town's Jon Walters.

PLYMOUTH ARGYLE
On This Day

APRIL

FRIDAY 1st APRIL 1938

Jack Tresadern was named as the new manager of Argyle. A former West Ham United player, Tresadern had made his England debut in 1923, and, in the same year, was part of the Hammers' side that lost to Bolton Wanderers in the first FA Cup final to be held at Wembley – although David Jack, the son of his predecessor as Argyle manager, Bob Jack, had scored twice for Bolton in the 2-0 Cup Final win. He retired from playing after breaking his leg, and, following management spells at Northampton Town, Crystal Palace and Spurs, took over at Argyle. He was in charge for one full season before the outbreak of war but returned to the club in 1945 – having served in the Army and rising to the rank of captain – and set about re-building the Argyle team and Home Park. He was sacked in 1947 after a disappointing start to the season.

TUESDAY 1st APRIL 2008

Argyle announced plans for a new tartan away kit for the 2008/09 season. It was said, fans had chosen the design in order to pay homage to manager Paul Sturrock – not to mention the large Scottish contingent on the Pilgrims' playing staff – but the Football Association scotched plans for the front of the shorts to carry a sporran motif, but a last-minute design alteration meant the kit would be completed with a much baggier style of shorts, mimicking the shape and flow of a kilt. The April Fools' Day prank caught out more than a few Argyle fans.

TUESDAY 2nd APRIL 1996

New signing Carlo Corazzin made a dramatic Home Park debut when he scored a late winner in the Pilgrims' 1-0 victory over Mansfield Town, keeping the club's Third Division promotion hopes alive. The Canadian international, a then-record £150,000 signing from Cambridge United, came off the substitutes' bench to win an injury-time penalty after being fouled. Then, quite bizarrely, manager Neil Warnock sent on instructions that Corazzin – whose last successful penalty had been against the Pilgrims – should take it, rather than Mark Patterson, who at the time was lining up the kick. Corazzin stepped up and duly converted the kick to secure a vital victory.

SATURDAY 2ND APRIL 1921

Argyle's Third Division (South) game against Southampton at Home Park ended in chaos when visiting goalkeeper Tommy Allen required a police escort to protect him from fans. Allen kept a clean sheet in the 0-0 draw but incurred the wrath of Pilgrims' supporters by manhandling Argyle winger Jimmy Kirkpatrick to the floor, necessitating medical treatment.

MONDAY 3RD APRIL 1972

Tragic striker Micky Cave made the last of his eight loan appearances from AFC Bournemouth in a 0-0 Third Division Home Park draw with Oldham Athletic. Cave scored twice on his debut to give the Pilgrims a 2-1 home victory over Rotherham United, the first of four goals before he returned to Dean Court. He later emigrated to coach in America, where he died from accidental carbon monoxide poisoning after running his car in a garage.

TUESDAY 3RD APRIL 2007

Argyle lost their Championship game at Burnley 4-0, the middle of three away defeats in eight days that manager Ian Holloway dubbed 'the Week from Hell' which ruined the Pilgrims' outside play-off hopes. Holloway was unequivocal about the performance at Turf Moor. "That was the worst performance of my football career," he said, after Burnley ended a 19-game winless streak.

THURSDAY 4TH APRIL 1929

Bob Wyllie was born in Dundee. Goalkeeper Wyllie played a small part in the Pilgrims' 1958/59 Third Division title success, standing in for Geoff Barnsley when Argyle's regular gloveman had to sit out five games because of injury towards the end of the season.

SATURDAY 4TH APRIL 1992

Peter Shilton became the oldest Argyle debutant when he made his first start in a 0-0 Second Division draw against Charlton at Upton Park. Shilton, who was 42 years and 199 days, had been brought to Home Park by chairman Dan McCauley in February 1992 as player-manager, but waited two months to fulfil the first part of his job description. As a player at Home Park, he made 41 appearances.

SATURDAY 5TH APRIL 1930

Former soldier Jack Vidler scored a hat-trick in a 4-0 home victory over Queens Park Rangers to take Argyle closer to the Third Division (South) title. The left-sided forward claimed seven hat-tricks in his 11-year Pilgrims' career, during which time he played 257 league games and scored 103 times. During the Second World War, Vidler played for the Bristol City team beaten 10-3 by the Pilgrims in a South West Regional League game at Home Park

SATURDAY 5TH APRIL 1986

Argyle set a post Second World War record of five consecutive away wins when they triumphed 3-1 at AFC Bournemouth on their way to promotion from the Third Division. Bristol Rovers, Wolves, Chesterfield and Cardiff City had already been dispatched by the Pilgrims on their travels. Striker Steve Cooper scored the first and made the second when he was bundled over to allow Russell Coughlin to net a penalty. Although John Beck pulled one back for the home side, Kevin Hodges restored Argyle's two-goal advantage.

SATURDAY 6TH APRIL 1963

Peter McParland scored a hat-trick as Argyle beat Leeds United 3-1 in a Second Division encounter at Home Park. The Northern Ireland international came to Plymouth with a huge reputation carved out as a winger with Aston Villa and Wolves. He scored five goals in the 1958 World Cup finals – before Northern Ireland lost to France in the quarter-final – after which McParland never re-appeared on the international scene. In two seasons at Home Park, he netted 14 goals.

SATURDAY 6TH APRIL 1974

Scottish midfielder Hughie Reed played his last Argyle game, a 3-0 Third Division defeat at Grimsby Town. Winger Reed scored eight goals in his first nine matches after arriving at Home Park in November 1971, including a flying header against Torquay United on Boxing Day that produced an iconic photograph. He could not live up to that start and was an irregular performer over the next couple of seasons.

SATURDAY 7TH APRIL 1956

Argyle's tenuous grip on the Second Division was wrenched from them by Bury, who won 7-1 at Gigg Lane. The game was gone as early as the 15th minute, by which time Bury were 3-0 ahead. Young Argyle goalkeeper Pete Dyer, making only his second appearance, had to pick the ball out of his net a further four times, and, although the 17-year-old from Devonport kept his place for the final two games of the campaign, he went on to make only four more starts.

SATURDAY 7TH APRIL 1979

Former Argyle midfielder Mick Horswill made an immediate impact on his return to Home Park with new side Hull City as he registered the quickest ever Home Park booking after just seven seconds. He was cautioned for a foul on Gary Megson as the Tigers went on to win the Third Division game 4-3.

SATURDAY 8TH APRIL 1933

The Greens' 'other' Black, Tommy, made his the first of his 168 Argyle appearances in a 1-0 Second Division home victory against Bury. For seven seasons, the names of Tommy and Sammy Black appeared together on the Argyle team-sheet, although they were not related. Wing-half Tommy arrived at Home Park from Arsenal, after literally being made a scapegoat and slung out of Highbury for conceding a successfully-converted penalty that gave Third Division Walsall a famous FA Cup win over the Gunners.

SATURDAY 9TH APRIL 1921

Forward Jimmy Heeps made the final of his 16 league appearances for Argyle. He scored just once, but it ensured his place in Pilgrims' history, coming in their first game as a Football League club. Heeps had been recruited from Scottish junior football especially for the Pilgrims' step up, and he stayed for a season before joining Airdrieonians.

SATURDAY 9TH APRIL 2005

After 12 consecutive defeats at the City Ground, Argyle won away to Nottingham Forest for the first time in 68 years when two goals from on-loan Southampton striker Dexter Blackstock spearheaded a memorable 3-0 win.

FRIDAY 10TH APRIL 1925

Jack Leslie scored a hat-trick as Argyle thrashed Bristol City 7-1 in the Third Division (South) at Home Park. Freddy Forbes notched a double.

SATURDAY 10TH APRIL 1926

Freddy Forbes and Jack Cock each scored twice as Argyle beat Luton Town 4-3 at Home Park on their way to promotion to the Second Division. The fourth goal was Argyle's 100th of the campaign, making them the first team to reach three figures in a single season, smashing Reading's previous best of 87.

SATURDAY 11TH APRIL 1908

Richard Morris became the first Argyle player to win a full international cap when he represented Wales in a 1-0 defeat by Ireland at the Athletic Ground, Aberdare.

SATURDAY 11TH APRIL 1953

Full-back George Robertson got the better of England legend Tommy Lawton in the Pilgrims' 1-0 Second Division victory over Brentford. Robertson was making his 13th appearance for the Greens against the vastly more experienced Lawton, and went on to play another 369 times for Argyle. After 14 years, he went on to be Home Park groundsman and, later, manager of the club's youth hostel.

SATURDAY 12TH APRIL 1969

Two down at home to Stockport County in the Third Division, Argyle fought back to draw 2-2 after team-mates Mike Bickle and Fred Molyneux fought on the pitch. Molyneux, a defender who had joined the attack, kept getting in Bickle's way and, when Bickle apprised him of this, the two got punchy. It did not stop Bickle scoring immediately after their contretemps, nor from Molyneux crossing to Bickle for the equaliser.

SATURDAY 12TH APRIL 1986

Dave Smith's promotion winners set a club record when they beat Bury 3-0 at Home Park –a ninth successive victory in a 35-day spell that had begun at Bristol Rovers on March 8. Kevin Hodges opened the scoring before a Tommy Tynan double. The match also saw the appearance of a small dog, inspiring a chorus of "There's Only One Jack Russell".

MONDAY 12TH APRIL 1993

Two days after an embarrassing 3-0 Second Division defeat by Exeter City at Home Park, Argyle won 5-2 at West Bromwich Albion, thanks to Steve Castle's hat-trick. Midfielder Castle ended the mid-table campaign as joint-leading scorer with 11 league goals.

SATURDAY 13TH APRIL 1912

Jack Boden scored a hat-trick as Argyle beat Reading 4-0 at Home Park in the Southern League. Despite the efforts of Boden, who scored 19 goals in 27 appearances that season, the Pilgrims ended the season as runners-up.

SATURDAY 13TH APRIL 2002

The Pilgrims unveiled a new tangerine away strip as they beat Carlisle United 2-0 at Brunton Park, thanks to goals from Marino Keith and Paul Wotton. With nearest rivals Luton Town being held 0-0 at home by Macclesfield Town, Argyle ended the afternoon needing two points from their final two games to win the Third Division.

SATURDAY 14TH APRIL 1956

Forward Bobby Bell, one of the first players to be loaned from one club to another, made his debut in a 3-1 Second Division home victory over Rotherham United. Bell was on National Service in Wiltshire and could not return to Scotland to play for his club, Partick Thistle, so Argyle and the Jags agreed to let him play the final two games of the season. Although he scored in the second, a 2-2 draw at Swansea, Argyle were relegated.

SATURDAY 14TH APRIL 1984

Argyle's only appearance in the FA Cup last four, and their bid to become the first Third Division side to reach the competition's Wembley final, ended in failure when First Division Watford beat John Hore's bravehearts 1-0 before nearly 44,000 people at Villa Park. George Reilly headed home a cross by John Barnes to score the only goal of the game. Argyle came no closer to equalising against Graham Taylor's side than in the final moments, when Kevin Hodges' low first-time left-foot shot appeared destined for the net before it bounced just the wrong side of the post.

TUESDAY 15TH APRIL 1975

Paul Mariner's 50th-minute goal ended Argyle's seven-year spell in the Third Division when it clinched promotion by way of a 1-0 win over Colchester United at Home Park. Their mid-table visitors' stubbornness was broken when Billy Rafferty seized on a mistake by U's goalkeeper Mike Walker to tee-up strike partner Mariner.

MONDAY 15TH APRIL 2002

Argyle won 4-0 against Darlington at Feethams to seal the Third Division title and claim their first championship for 43 seasons, having two days beaten Carlisle United earlier. The Pilgrims stayed in the north to play a game that had been snowed-off five weeks before, and the result was never in doubt from the tenth minute, when Michael Evans scored. The three points were in the bag following a Marino Keith double before half an hour, and a second-half strike from Jason Bent completed the victory. 'Que sera sera, whatever will be, will be," sang the Green Army "We're leaving Division Three."

TUESDAY 16TH APRIL 1974

Milija Aleksic, Spurs' 1981 FA Cup-winning goalkeeper, made his debut in a 1-0 Third Division victory over Charlton Athletic, two months after joining the Pilgrims from Stafford Rangers. Aleksic, whose father was Yugoslavian and mother English, had to wait for another season before trying to fill Jim Furnell's boots, but was offloaded to Luton Town after 32 league games. From there, he was picked up by Spurs where his reputation as an unlucky goalkeeper was enhanced when, in a Christmas game at Norwich City, he gashed his leg on a hook holding the net.

MONDAY 16TH APRIL 1990

Powerful centre-forward Sean McCarthy scored all three goals as Argyle won comfortably in a Second Division encounter at West Bromwich Albion 3-0. The Welsh striker returned to Home Park two days later to score both goals in a 2-0 win against Oldham Athletic, taking his tally to five in three days, and thus bagging nearly half of his goals scored in that nine-month season, inside the short space of just 72 hours.

SATURDAY 17TH APRIL 1999

Dwight Marshall, who had two spells at Argyle and was Pilgrims' Player of the Year in his debut 1991/92 season, made the last of his 147 appearances for the Greens in a 3-0 home Third Division defeat by Southend United. Jamaican-born Marshall played the bulk of his games in his first stint at Home Park between 1991 and 1994, making an immediate impact by scoring a debut winner in a 2-1 Second Division opening-day victory over Barnsley. Another 13 league goals followed that season, and 13 more in the two seasons after that, before he enjoyed an equally successful spell at Luton Town. He returned to Home Park for the 1998/99 campaign, scoring 12 league goals in 25 starts.

SATURDAY 17TH APRIL 2004

Argyle slid to a surpise 4-1 defeat at Oldham Athletic as the tension in the Second Division title race threatened to overcome them. They were already guaranteed at least a play-off place, but the unexpected hammering meant the Pilgrims had won just one of their previous six games. The game was noteworthy for the eccentric refereeing of Mike Cowburn, who sent off Pilgrims' goalscorer Paul Wotton. He also ruled out an Argyle goal for a push by Paul Connolly... on his own team-mate, Buster Phillips.

FRIDAY 18TH APRIL 1924

Full-back Billy Forbes made the last of his 141 Football League appearances for the Greens. Forbes, though, had been a Pilgrim for five seasons before they were promoted from the Southern League, having joined from Denny Hibernian in Scotland.

SATURDAY 18TH APRIL 1964

A point from a 1-1 draw with Leeds United at Elland Road denied the home side the Second Division title and helped Argyle survive in the division by a goal-average just 0.045 of a goal more than Grimsby Town. When the Pilgrims went 1-0 down to Willie Bell's deflected shot, everything was going according to the script before Welsh international goalkeeper Gary Sprake was lobbed by teenager Nicky Jennings for the equaliser. Leeds clinched the title the following week.

SATURDAY 19th APRIL 1930

Jack Vidler became the fifth Argyle player to score four goals in a league game when he fired Plymouth a step closer to winning the Third Division (South) title by hitting all four goals in an impressive 4-1 win over Norwich City at Home Park. Remarkably, all but the first came after he had been seriously injured. With Argyle leading from his early strike, Vidler was carried off the field following a collision with a Norwich defender and was diagnosed with severe concussion. He wasn't able to return to the field of play until ten minutes after half-time, and by then Norwich had levelled the scores. However, somewhere in his groggy haze, Vidler managed to focus long enough to net three more times.

SATURDAY 19th APRIL 1947

Bob Thomas scored a second-half hat-trick at the Hawthorns to give Argyle a surprise 5-2 Second Division victory over West Bromwich Albion. There was little sign of the carnage to come when the Pilgrims went 2-1 down shortly after half-time, their goal coming from Bill Strauss. Yet, after Strauss equalised for a second time, Thomas ended a personal goal-drought that stretched back to February 1 by netting three goals without any Albion reply.

MONDAY 19th APRIL 1954

Two goals in the last three minutes gave Argyle a 2-1 Easter Monday victory against West Ham at Home Park and helped them stay in the Second Division. West Ham's Tommy Dixon scored what looked like the match-winner in the 74th-minute and even Tony McShane's 87th-minute equaliser seemed no more than mere consolation. However, with seconds remaining, a fantastic solo goal from Johnny Porteous altered the course of Argyle's season.

SATURDAY 20th APRIL 1929

Two Sammy Black goals gave Argyle a 2-0 Third Division (South) victory over Luton at Home Park – the first win on a club record run of consecutive undefeated games that didn't end until some 22 matches later. It was not until Christmas Day the following season, in a match Coventry City at Highfield Road, that the Pilgrims tasted defeat again.

TUESDAY 20TH APRIL 2004

Bobby Williamson was appointed Argyle manager, succeeding Paul Sturrock four days before the Pilgrims clinched the Second Division title in the new man's first game. Sturrock was always going to be a hard act to follow for the Glaswegian, who had made his name as a coach north of the border with Kilmarnock, but he saw Argyle to safety in their first Coca-Cola Championship season. He was sacked after just six games of the 2005/06 campaign.

SATURDAY 21ST APRIL 1928

Goalkeeper Harry Cann made his Pilgrims' debut in a 2-2 Third Division (South) draw at Bournemouth & Boscombe Athletic. Cornishman Cann became the club's recognised number one when Fred Craig retired in 1930, and went on to make 225 league appearances.

SATURDAY 21ST APRIL 1979

Argyle's Third Division game against Gillingham was stopped after just ten minutes because of a spectator's coat. The yellow clothing was distracting a linesmen because it matched the shorts worn by the opposition players. Rather than move his place, the wearer of the coat removed it and was able to watch two Brian Johnson goals give the Pilgrims a 2-1 win.

MONDAY 22ND APRIL 1935

Two goals apiece from Jack Vidler and Frank Sloan helped the Pilgrims beat Nottingham Forest 5-2 in a Second Division game at Home Park. Sloan joined Argyle from Shieldmuir Celtic, made 240 appearances and scored 50 goals, and was one of many Pilgrims who returned to the club after their playing days, in his case, to work on the groundstaff.

SATURDAY 22ND APRIL 1967

Johnny Hore's goal from 30 yards three minutes from time earned Argyle a 2-1 win at Bolton Wanderers and ensured Second Division survival. It was Hore's first goal – he went on to score another 16 during his 400-game league career – in a feisty match controlled by future World Cup final referee Jack Taylor. Alan Banks' header gave Argyle the lead but Bolton immediately levelled through Ron Phillips.

WEDNESDAY 23RD APRIL 1952

Gordon Astall got the winner in the Pilgrims' 3-2 away defeat of Brighton to clinch promotion from Third Division (South). Appropriately enough for the date, George Dews netted Argyle's first after the Sussex side took the lead. Alex Govan headed the Pilgrims ahead, only for Brighton to level again, before the man known to the Green Army as 'Flash' struck.

SATURDAY 23RD APRIL 1988

Winger Dougie Anderson made the last of his 21 Argyle appearances in a 3-1 Second Division home defeat by Crystal Palace. Hong Kong-born Anderson had been brought from Tranmere Rovers as Garry Nelson's replacement but the task proved tough and, after failing to hold down a regular place, he returned to Hong Kong for a spell with the fragrantly-named Double Flower.

SATURDAY 24TH APRIL 1976

Phil Burrows, left-back in the Pilgrims' 1974/75 Third Division promotion-winning side, made his final Argyle appearance in a 2-0 Second Division defeat at Carlisle United. Burrows was signed by Tony Waiters after 333 league games for York City and was a virtual ever-present in the Greens' back line for two seasons, racking up 92 matches and scoring three times.

SATURDAY 24TH APRIL 2004

Argyle clinched the Second Division title with a 2-0 victory over promotion rivals Queens Park Rangers at Home Park. Rangers, managed by future Pilgrims' manager Ian Holloway, were nine minutes from a goalless draw when David Norris crossed for Michael Evans to head home at the Devonport end, and David Friio added a second five minutes later to secure promotion. With Bristol City failing to beat Brighton & Hove Albion, the title was Argyle's, too.

SATURDAY 25TH APRIL 1925

Argyle effectively lost the Third Division (South) title when they drew 1-1 with Swansea Town at Home Park in the season's penultimate match. Victory over their rivals would have all but guaranteed the Pilgrims – who had a superior goal-average – the championship. Freddy Forbes gave them an early lead which was quickly levelled by Harry Deacon.

SATURDAY 25TH APRIL 1998

Chris Billy, Argyle's Player of the Year in 1996/97, made his last appearance for the Pilgrims in a 1-0 home Second Division defeat by Gillingham, the penultimate game before the Pilgrims were relegated. Billy had followed former Huddersfield Town manager Neil Warnock to Home Park in the summer of 1996, having scored the Terriers' winner in the previous season's Second Division Play-Off Final. He gained promotion for the second season running as Argyle won the Third Division Play-Off Final, although, this time, he was a non-playing substitute at Wembley. After 131 games and eight goals, Billy rejoined Warnock at Bury.

SATURDAY 26TH APRIL 1947

A 2-0 Second Division loss to Birmingham City at Home Park began a joint club-record nine consecutive defeats. The Pilgrims plunged from 12th place to 19th as they lost the final six games of the season including a last-day 5-1 thrashing at Nottingham Forest. They began the subsequent campaign with a 6-1 drubbing at Newcastle United and it was not until the fourth game of the season that they stopped the rot with a 0-0 draw at home to Leicester City.

SATURDAY 26TH APRIL 1975

Argyle went down 1-0 at Peterborough United in the final game of the season, and, with defeat, lost the Third Division title to Blackburn Rovers by a point. The Pilgrims had gone into the game top and were already guaranteed promotion, but the 43-goal strike partnership of Paul Mariner and Billy Rafferty fired only blanks.

TUESDAY 27TH APRIL 1954

Argyle left from Southampton on the Ile De France for a 44-day summer tour of the USA. Thirteen of those days were spent crossing the Atlantic. The Pilgrims had 31 days in America, playing 10 matches in New York, Chicago, St Louis, Denver, Hollywood, San Francisco, Detroit and Philadelphia. They won eight and lost two. During the tour, goalkeeper Bill Shortt was loaned to fellow tourists Chelsea, who agreed to play a friendly at Home Park for the favour.

SATURDAY 27TH APRIL 1963

Argyle ended the season in record-breaking form, losing their final two games of the Second Division season to start a club-worst 13 games without winning. The streak began with a 3-0 defeat at Luton Town, before, four days later, they went down 2-1 at Cardiff City. It was October 12th the following season when the Pilgrims next won a league game, having started the campaign with a 5-0 defeat at Middlesbrough and experiencing another five defeats and five draws.

SATURDAY 28TH APRIL 1962

Argyle lost 3-2 to Liverpool in a Second Division game at Home Park that was – and probably always will be – the Reds' last ever win outside the top-flight. Cliff Jackson and George Robertson scored the goals.

SATURDAY 28TH APRIL 2007

Argyle beat Preston North End 2-0 at Home Park, with goals by Sylvan Ebanks-Blake, from the penalty spot, and Barry Hayles. Before the final home game of the Championship season, Lilian Nalis was named Player of the Season.

WEDNESDAY 29TH APRIL 1925

Argyle ended the Third Division (South) season with a 6-0 thrashing of Southend United at Home Park but missed out on promotion by a point, finishing runners-up – to Swansea Town – for the fourth season in succession. Patsy Corcoran netted twice and Sammy Black, Jack Leslie, Jack Cock and Freddy Forbes all scored.

WEDNESDAY 29TH APRIL 1959

A 1-1 draw at home to Bradford City clinched the first combined Third Division title. Wilf Carter's 22nd league goal ensured a crowd of 26,717 saw the Pilgrims finish one point ahead of Hull City. Had Argyle lost, they would have missed the championship on goal-average.

SATURDAY 29TH APRIL 1978

Argyle ensured their Third Division status by beating Port Vale 3-2 at Home Park, despite going behind inside two minutes. Fred Binney netted twice to achieve the victory they needed to avoid dropping into the Fourth Division for the first time.

TUESDAY 29TH APRIL 1986

A packed Home Park saw the Pilgrims clinch promotion to the Second Division with a 4-0 victory over Bristol City. Tommy Tynan, in a second spell at Argyle on loan from Rotherham United, opened the scoring after half an hour and, afterwards, there was no denying the Greens. Garry Nelson added number two and Russell Coughlin netted direct from a corner before Tynan scored his ninth goal in eight games.

WEDNESDAY 30TH APRIL 1952

Argyle lost their final Third Division (South) game of the season – 3-0 at Norwich City – but were already assured of only the second title in their history, 22 years after the first. Goal-power had been the Pilgrims' trump card, with 107 successful strikes in 46 games: Maurice Tadman led the way with 27 goals, George Dews was just behind with 25, Peter Rattray hit 19, and Gordon Astall 18.

SATURDAY 30TH APRIL 1955

A 2-0 victory over Stoke City at Home Park ensured Argyle's Second Division survival, and ruined the visitors' chances of promotion. George Willis and Hughie McJarrow scored as the Pilgrims stayed up at the expense of Ipswich Town and Derby County.

SUNDAY 30TH APRIL 2006

There was barely a dry eye at Home Park as Michael Evans brought down the curtain on an Argyle career that spanned 15 years and contained 81 goals from 432 league games. The 81st was also Argyle's last of their best season for nearly two decades, the winner in a 2-1 defeat of Ipswich Town. It came in the 57th minute after Pilgrim Tony Capaldi had cancelled out Nicky Forster's early opener. When Evans was substituted late in the game, every Argyle player – including goalkeeper Romain Larrieu – shook his hand. He returned for a post-match lap of honour, when the emotion pouring from the stands overwhelmed him and the tears flowed.

PLYMOUTH ARGYLE
On This Day

MAY

FRIDAY 1st MAY 1964

Malcolm Allison succeeded Andy Beattie as Argyle manager but, despite refreshing new tactics and guiding the Second Division Pilgrims to the semi-final of the League Cup, he lasted less than a season at Home Park. The crunch came in the penultimate home game of the 1964/65 campaign, when the directors insisted Allison select goalkeeper John Leiper ahead of Noel Dwyer.

SATURDAY 1st MAY 1965

Malcolm Allison's successor as manager was his right-hand man at Home Park, and former Charlton Athletic team-mate, Derek Ufton, who held the post – his only as manager – for nearly three years. A centre-half with one England cap during his playing days, Ufton also played first-class cricket for Kent where he was understudy to Godfrey Evans. After leaving Argyle, Ufton remained close to both his sporting loves, becoming a director of the Addicks and chairman of cricket at Kent.

SUNDAY 1st MAY 1977

Mike Kelly preceded Malcolm Allison's second spell as Argyle manager, taking over from Tony Waiters – like Kelly, a former goalkeeper – just before the end of a season which ended in relegation to the Third Division. Kelly, who had been Waiters' reserve-team manager, could not halt the Pilgrims' slide and resigned after less than a season in charge.

SATURDAY 2nd MAY 1931

Tommy Grozier hit a hat-trick as Argyle rounded off their first season in the Second Division with a 5-3 victory over Bristol City at Home Park. Winger Grozier, a Scot who had joined the Pilgrims from Glencairn in 1927, ended the campaign with 15 goals from 39 appearances.

SATURDAY 2nd MAY 1953

Argyle went down 4-0 away at Huddersfield Town on the final day of the season but still finished fourth in the Second Division table for their joint-best ever finishing position, emulating the 1931/32 team. Coincidentally, both sides amassed 49 points from 42 games. Argyle had been champions of Third Division (South) only 12 months previously.

SATURDAY 2ND MAY 1998

A 2-1 defeat by Burnley at Turf Moor condemned Argyle to relegation to the Third Division. A point would have kept the Pilgrims up, and sent Chris Waddle's side down. Things were going Argyle's way when Mark Saunders levelled Andy Cooke's early strike, but Cooke added a second before half-time to send Mick Jones' side down.

SATURDAY 3RD MAY 1924

Frank Sloan hit the first of his two Argyle hat-tricks in a 7-1 home thrashing of Southend United as Plymouth ended the season as runners-up in the Third Division (South). Jack Leslie scored twice, as did Percy Cherrett, who finished the campaign as leading scorer with 27 goals.

SATURDAY 3RD MAY 1930

Nine seasons after joining the Football League, and having finished runners-up in the Third Division (South) six times, the Pilgrims finally celebrated winning the title with a 2-1 victory over Watford at Home Park. A giant pasty was presented to Argyle captain Fred Titmuss and then laid behind one of the goals before a game which the Pilgrims won with goals from Frank Sloan and Sammy Black.

SATURDAY 3RD MAY 1997

Argyle ended the 1996/97 season with a 0-0 Second Division draw at home to AFC Bournemouth to begin a club-record five consecutive drawn matches. The Pilgrims opened the following campaign by drawing 1-1 with Bristol Rovers; were held 2-2 at home by Grimsby Town; shared two goals at Wigan Athletic; and did likewise at Home Park when Chesterfield visited. A 1-0 home defeat by Watford three days later broke the sequence.

SATURDAY 4TH MAY 1946

Argyle beat Nottingham Forest 3-2 at Home Park to register their third win of the first season after the Second World War. Bob Thomas scored the winner and goalkeeper George Wright saved a penalty. The Pilgrims finished the campaign bottom, a position partly explicable by the fact that they used 72 players, a third of which were 'guests' who did not play more than one or two games each.

SATURDAY 4TH MAY 1996

Argyle missed promotion to the Second Division after their first season in the lowest tier of the professional game, despite beating Hartlepool United 3-0 at Home Park. Chris Billy, Mick Heathcote and Richard Logan scored but the win left Neil Warnock's Argyle having to settle for the play-offs as they finished fourth, a point behind Bury.

SATURDAY 5TH MAY 1979

Swansea City goalkeeper Geoff Crudgington helped the Swans to promotion thanks to a 2-2 Third Division draw at Home Park in which Argyle twice led, through Player of the Year Fred Binney and Brian Bason. Alan Curtis and John Toshack scored for Swansea, who would not have gone up if they had lost. The following season, Crudgington joined Argyle to begin a long and distinguished Pilgrims' career as player and coach.

SATURDAY 5TH MAY 2001

Defender Paul Connolly, goalkeeper Luke McCormick and forward Ryan Trudgian made their Football League debuts in a 0-0 home Third Division draw against Rochdale on the final day of the 2000/01 season, a result that denied the opposition a play-off place. Of the three, only substitute Trudgian failed to kick on – this was his only taste of first-team action.

SATURDAY 6TH MAY 1950

Argyle were relegated for the first time in their history despite a 2-0 home victory over Bury on the final day of the season. Goals from Eric Bryant and Paddy Blatchford could halt the Pilgrims' drop from the Second Division, 20 seasons after first winning promotion.

TUESDAY 6TH MAY 1975

Argyle lost 4-3 at home to Liverpool in a testimonial game for long-serving former captain and future manager John Hore, who played exactly 400 league games for the Pilgrims between his debut in April 1965 and his final bow in October 1975. Billy Rafferty, John Delve, and Paul Mariner scored on Cornishman Hore's big night... but he was not finished. After leaving Home Park, he hopped up the A38 and made more than 200 appearances for Exeter City.

SATURDAY 7th MAY 1938

Bill Hullett scored the first of three hat-tricks in seven games as Argyle ended their Second Division campaign with a 4-0 victory over Southampton at Home Park. The Liverpudlian scored another two triples in the opening six games of the subsequent campaign.

SATURDAY 7th MAY 1932

Argyle beat Chesterfield 4-0 at Home Park to secure their joint-best league finish; fourth in the Second Division. Joe Mantle, Sammy Black, Jack Leslie and Ray Bowden scored the goals and Bowden rounded things off by netting the 100th league goal of the campaign – only champions Wolves scored more. Argyle finished level on 49 points from 42 games with Bury and Bradford PA but boasted a superior goal-average.

SATURDAY 7th MAY 1977

A 1-0 defeat at Sheffield United sealed Argyle's relegation to the Third Division after two seasons in the Second. Teenage striker Keith Edwards, who enjoyed a short loan spell at Home Park much later, scored the goal that put Argyle down. The sale of Paul Mariner during the season, and the sacking of manager Tony Waiters four matches before the end, did not help the Pilgrims, who lost five of their last six games.

SATURDAY 7th MAY 1994

Argyle recorded their biggest away league victory and equalled their best league score, home or away, set 62 years earlier, when they won 8-1 at Hartlepool United on the final day of the Second Division season. Richard Landon scored a hat-trick and Paul Dalton netted twice against the already-relegated north-easterners. However, Port Vale's simultaneous victory at Brighton & Hove Albion denied the third-placed Pilgrims automatic promotion.

SATURDAY 8th MAY 1999

Argyle were the fall guys as Carlisle United goalkeeper Jimmy Glass scored to give the Cumbrians a 2-1 Third Division home win in the final minute of the 1998/99 season and keep them in the Football League. The goal was ranked seventh in *The Times'* list of the 50 most important goals in football history.

SATURDAY 8TH MAY 2004

Argyle rounded off their Second Division title-winning season by beating Colchester United 2-0 at Home Park. Goals from David Friio and David Norris secured the victory. Friio was later sent off for handling Kem Izzet's effort on the goal-line but, with Scott McGleish missing the resultant penalty, the Pilgrims hung on to register an impressive 26th victory and equally impressive 21st clean-sheet of the campaign.

SUNDAY 8TH MAY 2005

David Worrell made his final appearance in a green shirt as the Pilgrims brought the curtain down on their first-ever Championship season with a 0-0 draw at home to Leicester City. Worrell was one of Paul Sturrock's first signings as manager, from Dundee United in 2000, and the Dubliner went on to play more than 150 league and Cup games for the Pilgrims, featuring in the promotion sides of 2001/02 and 2003/04.

SUNDAY 9TH MAY 1954

Neil Langman scored a double hat-trick as Argyle won the second game of their US tour 8-4 against the St Louis All Stars in St Louis. Among the items Argyle players packed for their Stateside stay was half a gallon of olive oil, to keep limbs supple.

FRIDAY 9TH MAY 1958

Argyle played a combined West Cornwall side in Helston in a money-making post-season friendly, with all proceeds of the game being donated to the Manchester United Disaster Fund set up in the wake of the tragic Munich aeroplane crash earlier that year.

SATURDAY 10TH MAY 1947

Full-back Bob Royston made his final Argyle appearance in a 1-0 Second Division defeat at Newport County. Geordie Royston was signed by the Pilgrims from Southport at the end of the 1938/39 season and played just five games before war interrupted the Football League fixtures. After the 1946/47 season, during which he captained the Greens and made another 37 appearances, he retired from the game.

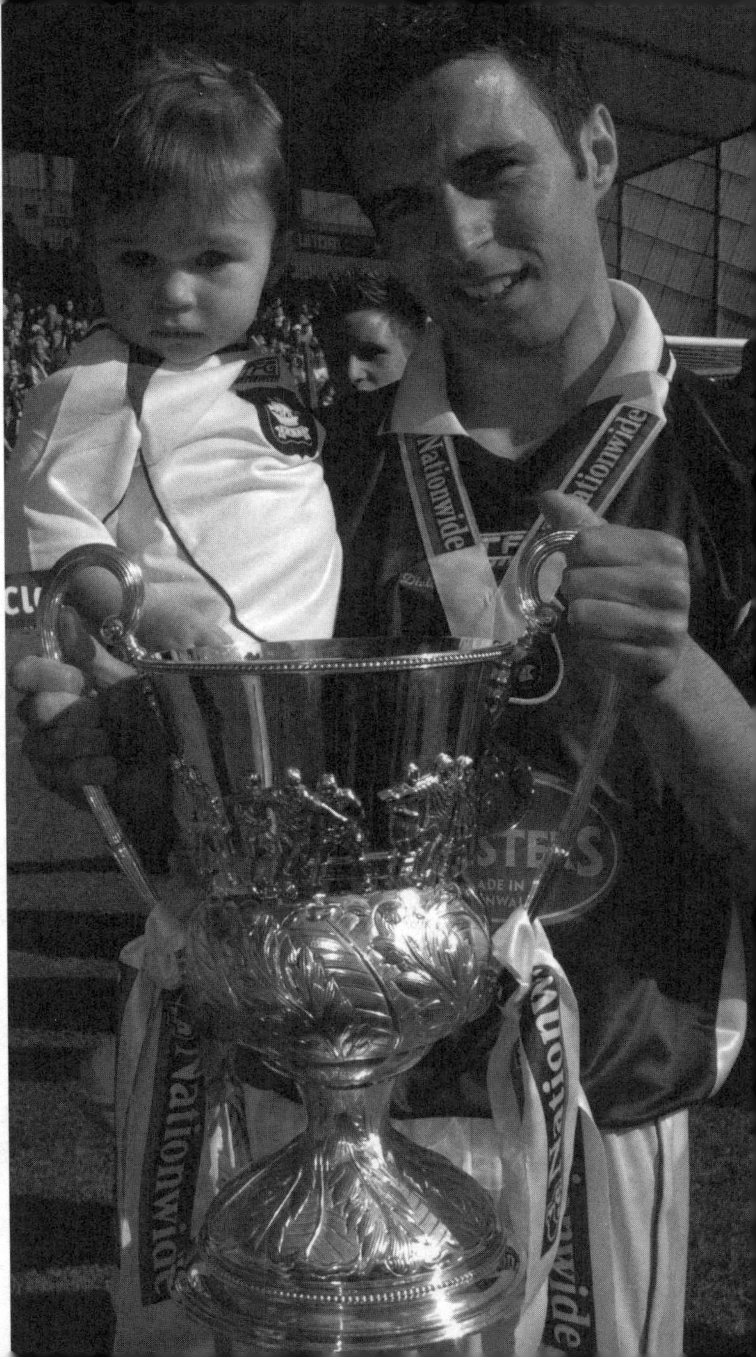

DAVID WORRELL: SEE 8th MAY 2005

SATURDAY 11TH MAY 1985

Defender Chris Harrison made the last of his 371 Argyle appearances in a 2-0 Third Division defeat at Millwall, nine years after his debut. The crowd at the Den – 1,346 – is the lowest the Pilgrims have played in front of in the Football League. Launceston-born Harrison played under seven different Argyle managers, and, from 1979 to 1984, he hardly missed a game, including the 1983/84 run to the semi-final of the FA Cup. A season later, he was given a free transfer by Dave Smith in recognition of his service to the Pilgrims.

SATURDAY 12TH MAY 1984

Neville Chamberlain, the less well-known but more famously-named brother of England forward Mark, played the last of 11 games on loan from Stoke City. Chamberlain scored three times in seven starts as the Pilgrims fought a rearguard action against relegation from the Third Division.

SUNDAY 12TH MAY 1996

Argyle lost 1-0 at Colchester United in the first leg of the Third Division play-off semi-final. A goal by midfielder Mark Kinsella just before half-time was the difference between the two sides. It gave Colchester a second home victory over Neil Warnock's side, having also won 2-1 at Layer Road on the opening day of the campaign.

MONDAY 13TH MAY 1940

Len Rich scored a hat-trick on his fifth – and last – appearance for the Greens as they won a home South West Regional League game 4-1 against Bristol Rovers. Rich had played three games for Argyle in the 1935/36 season before leaving for spells at Luton Town and Exeter City, but returned to Home Park during the war. He scored on his second 'debut' – a 2-2 draw at Swindon Town – before bowing out in style.

THURSDAY 13TH MAY 1954

Sam McCrory matched Neil Langman by scoring a double hat-trick on Argyle's tour of America as the Pilgrims beat the Colorado All Stars 16-2 in Denver. Langman added another two, and there were other doubles from Jimmy Crawford and substitute Ernie Edds.

SUNDAY 14TH MAY 1944

Keith Etheridge, a forward plucked from non-league football, was born, in Ivybridge. Etheridge joined the Pilgrims from Cornish side St Blazey and debuted on the opening day of the 1966/67 season. However he did not cement his place in the side until February, when he scored two goals in a 4-2 defeat at Hull City. Four more goals in nine more games followed, and he played 18 league matches without scoring in the subsequent campaign before joining Southern League Weymouth.

SATURDAY 14TH MAY 1983

Portsmouth claimed the Third Division title with a 1-0 victory over Argyle at Home Park, a match blighted by the hooliganism of visiting supporters which caused hundreds of pounds worth of damage and had Argyle fans running for safety even before the game had begun. Denis Law lookalike Alan Biley scored Pompey's goal just before the hour to achieve the result that the police and even Argyle's own officials accepted as the best possible in the circumstances, although a draw, or even a narrow defeat, would still have given the visitors the title.

WEDNESDAY 15TH MAY 1963

Argyle's short four-game visit to Poland and East Germany got off to a terrible start, without a ball even being kicked. After arriving in Warsaw, Argyle found themselves housed in poor accommodation – not the promised Hotel Europejski – and unable to upgrade because the city was awash with thousands of people attending the 16th International Cycle Race for Peace. A threatened walk-out was averted by apologetic tour operators.

SUNDAY 15TH MAY 1994

Argyle recorded an impressive 0-0 draw against Burnley at Turf Moor in the first leg of the Second Division play-off semi-final, having lost the league encounter at Turf Moor 4-2 earlier in the season. This time, Peter Shilton's Pilgrims survived with a draw, despite having Adrian Burrows sent off. The goalless draw was enough to make Shilton's side favourites to win the tie overall and secure a first-ever visit to Wembley.

WEDNESDAY 15TH MAY 1996

Two seasons after messing up a golden opportunity to win through to the Play-Off Final, Argyle finally reached Wembley for the first time in their history, thanks to a 3-1 second-leg victory over Colchester United in the Third Division semi-final gave them a 3-2 aggregate triumph. Michael Evans made the score 1-1 on aggregate after three minutes, and Chris Leadbitter's 41st minute free-kick put the Greens ahead. With Argyle manager Neil Warnock on the terraces – having been banished from the dug-out by referee John Kirkby – Mark Kinsella levelled the aggregate score. However, Paul Williams headed home a Martin Barlow 85th minute cross to win the tie.

SUNDAY 16TH MAY 1954

Argyle lost to Borussia Dortmund for the second time on their American tour, going down 3-1 in Los Angeles despite Sam McCrory scoring for the third successive match. Afterwards, the players visited the Paramount Film studios and met Western star Audie Murphy.

THURSDAY 16TH MAY 1963

The largest crowd ever to watch an Argyle game saw the Pilgrims lose 2-1 to Legia Warsaw in front of 100,000 people at the Warsaw Stadium. The Pilgrims, for whom Wilf Carter scored against the Polish Army team, were not the main attraction: the game was stopped three times as participants in the Prague-Warsaw-Berlin 16th International Cycle Race for Peace entered the stadium, and loudspeakers blared out the positions of the cyclists throughout the match.

SATURDAY 17TH MAY 1947

Pat Jones, who sits third on the list of names in Argyle's exclusive five-man 400-club, made his debut in a 1-0 Second Division defeat at Coventry City. Defender Jones overcame an unpromising start to his Argyle career when he took part in nine winless games in which the opposition scored 26 goals, before tasting victory and going on to make 425 league appearances for the Greens. Only Sammy Black and Kevin Hodges have played more games than the Plymothian left-back whose career spanned 12 seasons. He did not miss a single match in five of those seasons.

MONDAY 17TH MAY 2004

Paul Sturrock was named as the Second Division manager of the season by the League Managers' Association. Despite leaving the Pilgrims for Southampton with 12 matches of the 2003/04 season remaining, Sturrock's input was enough for him to garner a majority of the votes from the Second Division managers, and he was presented with the award at the annual LMA dinner.

SATURDAY 18TH MAY 1963

Another huge crowd saw the Pilgrims go down 1-0 in the second of a four-game tour behind the Iron Curtain. This time, 60,000 people witnessed a 1-0 win for KSC Lech in Poznan. The match-ball had been dropped from a helicopter as the teams lined up before the game, but it was found to be too soft and another had to be used.

WEDNESDAY 18TH MAY 1994

Having secured a goalless draw at Turf Moor in the first-leg of the Second Division play-off semi-final against Burnley, Argyle saw the Twin Towers come into focus when Dwight Marshall put them ahead in the second leg at Home Park – but then everything went horribly wrong as Argyle imploded in spectacular fashion. Two goals from John Marshall and a killer third by former Argyle captain Warren Joyce meant no first trip to Wembley for the Pilgrims and obviously no promotion – a cruel end to a decent season. Both went to Burnley – who beat Stockport County 2-1 in the Wembley showpiece. The Clarets had finished 14 points behind both Argyle and Stockport in the regular season.

SUNDAY 18TH MAY 1997

Argyle overcame the extreme heat and soaring temperatures in excess of 100 degrees to beat the Gambian National side 2-1 in a post-season trip to Africa. To a background of the rhythmic beating of African drums, the Pilgrims scored twice from set-pieces. The first was set up by captain Mick Heathcote for Richard Logan, and the second came after the Gambian goalkeeper failed to collect a corner from Martin Barlow, leaving Mark Patterson free to head home at the far post. The most expensive seats in the ground cost only ten dalasi, which coverted to around 70 pence in sterling.

TUESDAY 19TH MAY 1896

Forward William Toms, who scored five goals in Argyle's inaugural Football League season, was born in Manchester. Toms joined the Pilgrims from Manchester United, and his first league goal came in November's 5-0 trouncing of Brighton & Hove Albion. Four others followed in his 29 appearances, including FA Cup strikes against Swansea Town and Chelsea.

THURSDAY 19TH MAY 2005

Hungarian midfielder Ákos Buzsáky said it was a "dream come true" after signing for the Pilgrims following a 15-game loan spell at Home Park the previous spring. "I came for only three months last season, but these three months were the best in my career – until today," said the player who became a fans' favourite in his 105 games at Home Park.

SUNDAY 20TH MAY 1888

Moses Russell, one of Argyle's most capped internationals, was born, in Tredegar. Former miner Russell signed for Argyle in 1914 and played his last game in 1930. He won 23 international caps and toured Canada with the Welsh side in 1929, when a member of the crowd pointed a pistol at him after a pitch invasion during a game in Hamilton, Ontario.

THURSDAY 20TH MAY 1954

Game number five on the Pilgrims' summer tour of the USA saw victory number three, a 2-0 win over the Los Angeles Scots All Stars in LA. Malcolm Davies and supersub Ernie Edds scored Argyle's goals. The price of admission to the matches on the tour was between $1 and $1.50.

TUESDAY 21ST MAY 1963

Argyle registered the first win of their eight-day tour of Poland and East Germany when they beat BWKS Lechia 3-0 in Gdansk. Wilf Carter, Jimmy McAnearney and Alan O'Neill scored for the Pilgrims, who were housed in the Grand Hotel in Sopot. Goalkeeper Dave MacLaren, also a pianist, led the party in a selection of songs to entertain the guests after breakfast.

FRIDAY 21st MAY 2004

The club held its Centenary Ball to celebrate 100 years as a professional club. The Argyle Team of the Century, as voted for by the club's supporters, was the centrepiece of the occasion in Plymouth Guildhall. The team, 4-4-2 style, was: Jim Furnell; Gordon Nisbet, Jack Chisholm, Graham Coughlan, Colin Sullivan; Kevin Hodges, Johnny Williams, Ernie Machin, Sammy Black or Garry Nelson; Tommy Tynan, Paul Mariner. Manager: Paul Sturrock.

THURSDAY 22nd MAY 1969

Winger Mark Robson, who made his Argyle debut in a 2-2 Home Park draw against West Bromwich Albion on Boxing Day 1989, was born, in Newham. Robson started at Exeter City before being transferred to Tottenham Hotspur, from where Ken Brown borrowed him for Argyle to give a flagging 1989/90 Second Division campaign momentum. He played seven games before returning to Spurs.

SUNDAY 23rd MAY 1954

Argyle's coast-to-coast tour of USA reached San Francisco, where the Pilgrims beat San Francisco 3-2 thanks to two goals from Johnny Porteous and one from Neil Langman. Pat Jones received abdominal injuries that kept him out of the remainder of the tour and made the subsequent seven-hour 1,900 mile trip to Chicago even more arduous.

THURSDAY 23rd MAY 1963

Argyle's end-of-season tour behind the Iron Curtain moved to East Germany and a 3-2 defeat by SC Turbine in Erfurt, where Mike Trebilcock and Peter McParland scored. The Pilgrims had to cope with temperatures of 86 degrees in front of another 40,000-plus crowd.

SATURDAY 24th MAY 1969

Defender Richard Logan, a key member of Neil Warnock's 1995/96 promotion-winning team, was born in Barnsley. Logan signed from Huddersfield Town, bringing to six the number of ex-Terriers at Home Park who had won promotion to the First Division the previous season, joining Warnock, assistant Mick Jones, Kevin Blackwell, Gary Clayton and Chris Billy. Logan scored six goals in 25 league games as the Pilgrims went up, and went on to make 94 appearances.

TUESDAY 25TH MAY 1954

Argyle hit eight in the seventh game of their summer tour of the United States, beating the Chicago All Stars 8-1 at Wrigley Field. Paddy Ratcliffe, Sam McCrory and Neil Dougall notched a brace apiece. The Pilgrims were greeted in the Windy City by former Argyle player Jimmy Cook, who left the Pilgrims for the States in 1909 and rose to become president of the Kloster Steel Corporation of Chicago.

SATURDAY 25TH MAY 1996

Argyle's only appearance at the old Wembley ended in promotion to the Second Division as Neil Warnock's side beat Darlington 1-0 in the Third Division Play-Off Final. A headed goal from midfielder Ronnie Maugé was the difference between the two sides, the result of a well-worked corner routine that saw defender Mark Patterson provide the cross for the goal. It was a fitting end to a campaign that had seen Maugé score the Pilgrims' very first goal under Warnock in a friendly at Tiverton nearly 11 months previously.

SATURDAY 26TH MAY 2007

Saturday night was alright for Argyle, who staged their first-ever pop concert when Sir Elton John headlined in front of 22,000 people at Home Park. Sir Elton played a two and a half hour set of 24 songs that included 'Benny and the Jets', 'Rocket Man' and 'Crocodile Rock', and even, at one point, wore an Argyle scarf thrown up to him onstage.

MONDAY 27TH MAY 1901

The Argyle Athletic Club staged their first event at Home Park, a Whit Monday athletics meeting, after obtaining a lease from the city council. The possession of such a good ground helped the Pilgrims' application to turn professional and saw them gain entry to the Southern League two years later.

MONDAY 27TH MAY 2002

Argyle announced that David Tall was to step down as the Pilgrims' chief executive and take up a brand-new post of Strategic and Development Officer.

WEDNESDAY 28TH MAY 2008

A group of under-15 and under-14 Argyle stars of the future arrived in Latvia for a tournament against the international teams of Latvia and Belarus. The Centre of Excellence trip was a reciprocal arrangement following the Latvian youth team's visit to Plymouth the previous August, when the under-18s won 8-2 over two legs in the Duchy College Cup.

SATURDAY 29TH MAY 1954

On the first Saturday afternoon game of their USA summer tour, Argyle beat the Chicago Polish Falcons 6-1 in Detroit, with Sam McCrory (2), Jimmy Crawford (2), Ernie Edds and Neil Langman scoring. The party was joined in Detroit by club chairman Sir Clifford Tozer after the end of his term as Lord Mayor of Plymouth.

SATURDAY 30TH MAY 1903

Argyle obtained professional status, thanks to the efforts of Clarence Spooner, a local businessman who bought Home Park and recruited a Royal Artillery Captain Frederick Windrum to lead the drive for professional registration. Windrum had previously been instrumental in registering Portsmouth as a professional team.

SUNDAY 30TH MAY 1954

Another day and another victory over an American select team. This time it was the Philadelphia All-Stars who were beaten 3-2 in Philadelphia in the penultimate game of the Pilgrims' US tour, with Paddy Ratcliffe, Jimmy Crawford and Neil Langman scoring.

SATURDAY 31ST MAY 1947

Argyle's season ended disappointingly with a 5-1 Second Division defeat at Nottingham Forest. The Pilgrims ended the campaign with four successive away games, all of which ended in defeat, and lost 11 of their last 12 games, tumbling from ninth to 19th in the process.

SATURDAY 31ST MAY 1930

Argyle celebrated winning the Third Division (South) title with a tour of the city, followed by a celebration dinner at the Duke of Cornwall Hotel. WS Tonkin, author of *All About Argyle*, reported: "It seemed that the whole population of Plymouth turned out to express their jubilation."

PLYMOUTH ARGYLE
On This Day

JUNE

TUESDAY 1st JUNE 1954

A Neil Langman goal brought the curtain down on a successful tour of America by Argyle, giving the Pilgrims a 1-0 win over the American All-Stars in New York. Langman's goal was the Greens' 48th of the ten-game coast-to-coast trip.

MONDAY 1st JUNE 1981

Bobby Moncur was appointed Argyle manager. Moncur came to Argyle with an impressive CV, having won 16 Scottish caps as a player, and captained Newcastle United to victory in the Inter-Cities Fairs Cup in 1969. He managed Carlisle United before moving to Hearts and winning the Scottish First Division in 1980. His spent just over two seasons at Home Park before leaving in 1983 – on the day Argyle beat Scunthorpe United 4-0 – after falling out with the board, who wanted him to buy John Aldridge from Newport County.

WEDNESDAY 2nd JUNE 1965

Midfielder David Campbell was born, in Derry. Campbell was borrowed by manager Ken Brown from Charlton Athletic for – as it turned out – one match; a 2-1 Second Division victory at Blackburn Rovers in March 1989. Immediately after the game, Campbell decided to cut short his supposed one-month loan to join Bradford City. Playing for Blackburn that afternoon was David Byrne, who, immediately after the game, finished his loan to join... Argyle.

WEDNESDAY 2nd JUNE 1999

Argyle signed Barrington Belgrave from Norwich City. Forward Belgrave made his debut, as a substitute, against Southend United, the club for which he would eventually leave the Pilgrims for, in a Third Division defeat at Roots Hall. After one more start, 16 substitute appearances, and no goals, his Pilgrims' career was over.

THURSDAY 3rd JUNE 2004

Scottish midfielder Keith Lasley joined Argyle from Motherwell. In two seasons at Home Park, Lasley made 32 appearances – half of them as a substitute – before returning to the Well, and starring in their 2007/08 Scottish Premier League campaign when they finished third behind champions Celtic.

THURSDAY 4TH JUNE 1992

Former Argyle youth trainee Ryan Cross made one of the longest transfers possible in English football when he left Home Park to sign for Hartlepool United. Plymothian Cross had made the last of his 21 league and Cup appearances for the Pilgrims a few weeks earlier, when they had lost 3-1 at home to Kenny Dalglish's Blackburn Rovers to be relegated from the old Second Division to the new Second Division.

SUNDAY 4TH JUNE 2000

Lincoln City captain Terry Fleming joined Argyle, having amassed more than 180 league appearances for the Imps in four and a half seasons. His stay at Argyle was at the other end of the scale. Signed by Kevin Hodges, the midfielder did not win over new manager Paul Sturrock, although he featured in his first Argyle side, and moved on to Cambridge United after 15 league starts.

SUNDAY 5TH JUNE 1921

Centre-forward George Dews, the most-famous cricketer to play for the club, was born, in Ossett. Dews made his Pilgrims' debut in a 1-1 Second Division draw at Chesterfield in November 1947 and played his final match eight years later, having scored 81 goals in 271 appearances. There would surely have been more games for Argyle had it not been for Dews' commitment to Worcestershire County Cricket Club – which meant he missed the start and end of each of the eight seasons he was registered as a player at Home Park. He made his Worcestershire debut before his Argyle one, in 1946, being dismissed for a pair. A right-handed batsman and an excellent fielder, he passed 1,000 runs for the season 11 times but was never picked for England.

MONDAY 6TH JUNE 1932

Argyle goalkeeper Jimmy Gee, who perhaps enjoyed more success as a Devon County water-polo player, was born in Plymouth. Gee made only one appearance for the Greens, as they sought a successor to Bill Shortt and Les Major, in a 3-0 Third Division (South) defeat at Queens Park Rangers in 1956. After the game, the amateur custodian returned whence he came: Launceston.

WEDNESDAY 6TH JUNE 1979

Another one-game wonder, Dean Crowe, who played for and against Argyle in their Third Division 2001/02 title-winning season, was born in Stockport. Crowe was a substitute in the Pilgrims' opening-day defeat by Shrewsbury Town at Home Park, before the on-loan Stoke City striker returned to the Potteries for "family reasons". Crowe then joined Luton Town and was the Hatters' scorer when the two sides met at Home Park soon afterwards. Argyle won 2-1.

FRIDAY 7TH JUNE 1940

Argyle played their penultimate game in the Second World War South West Regional League, losing 6-3 at Newport County, having already wrapped up the divisional title. Bill Archer scored a couple of the goals, and Billy Fellowes netted the other. Fellowes was guesting for the Pilgrims – having originally left Home Park in 1933 – from Exeter.

SATURDAY 8TH JUNE 1940

The Pilgrims completed their successful South West Regional League campaign with a 5-2 defeat at Newport County – Bill Archer and Charles Sargeant scored. Sargeant – who was, appropriately, called up for the Army soon after making his mark at Newport – never played League football for the Greens before or after the truncated 1939/40 season. It was the latest an Argyle season had ended.

MONDAY 9TH JUNE 1913

Len Jones, 'the Stanley Matthews of the Third Division', was born in Barnsley. Jones earned that sobriquet at Colchester United, where he converted from wing-half after playing at Home Park. Jones was one of the few who joined the Pilgrims before the Second World War and was still around afterwards. He made 38 league appearances between 1946 and 1949, and was still playing, for Colchester, in his forties – just like Sir Stanley.

WEDNESDAY 9TH JUNE 1954

Argyle returned to Plymouth after a 44-day post-season coast-to-coast tour of America, during which they travelled 14,000 miles by sea, air and land. The return transatlantic journey to Plymouth on the liner *Flandre* was rough, with most of the party suffering from seasickness.

THURSDAY 10TH JUNE 1965

Winger Phil Barber, who made his Argyle debut in 3-0 Second Division defeat at Swansea Town on Boxing Day 1994, was born. An FA Cup finalist and top-flight player with Crystal Palace, Barber played just four games on loan from Millwall towards the end of his career and was on the winning side just once. He was, however, at the club to witness the departure of the man who signed him, former England keeper Peter Shilton.

SUNDAY 11TH JUNE 1899

John Devine, a product of Scottish junior side Kilsyth Rangers, was born in Glasgow. Devine made his debut in a 3-1 Third Division (South) victory over Swansea Town at Home Park on New Year's Eve 1921 but, with his first-team path blocked by Moses Russell and Billy Forbes, played only 13 more times.

MONDAY 11TH JUNE 2007

Argyle lost their battle to continue using the old Mayflower Terrace at Home Park after the club's appeal to the government for special dispensation to keep the standing area open for a further 12 months was rejected. The Pilgrims later installed 3,500 seats on the terracing area to ensure fans could still view the action from that area of the ground.

SUNDAY 12TH JUNE 1960

Midfielder and Argyle stalwart Kevin Hodges was born in Broadwindsor, Dorset. He went onto make a club-record 620 senior appearances in all competitions for the Pilgrims between 1978 and 1992, after serving his Home Park apprenticeship. Hodges made his debut in a 2-1 Third Division victory at Bury in September 1978, the first of another club-record 530 league appearances in the green. He played in the 1984 FA cup semi-final, and was Player of the Year and leading goalscorer in the 1985/86 Third Division promotion-winning season. He was a shoo-in for the Centenary Season fans' Team of the Century. After a successful spell as player and manager at Torquay United, in which he took the Gulls to a Wembley Play-Off Final, Hodges returned to Home Park in 1998 and oversaw two mediocre, financially-troubled, seasons in which the Pilgrims finished mid-table in the Third Division.

TUESDAY 12TH JUNE 1934

Goalkeeper Dave MacLaren, who had to wait before becoming a Pilgrims' regular, was born in Auchterarder, Perthshire. He joined the Pilgrims in 1960 after having won promotion to the First Division with Leicester City but had to see off Geoff Barnsley before claiming the Argyle number one spot. He nailed the position until early 1965, making 131 league appearances in his five seasons, when former Pilgrims' manager Andy Beattie took him to Wolves.

FRIDAY 13TH JUNE 2003

Ex-Argyle captain Craig Taylor joined Torquay United on a free transfer from the Pilgrims. Defender Taylor made 98 appearances between 1998 and 2003 after signing from Swindon Town. However, he missed virtually the entire 2001-02 Third Division title-winning campaign after breaking his ankle in April of the previous season, making one appearance, at home to York City, as a substitute after David Worrell had been sent off.

SATURDAY 14TH JUNE 1969

Defender Richard Dryden was born in Stroud. Dryden played five games on loan at Home Park from Notts County in 1992. He joined Exeter City (manager Terry Cooper) in March 1989 and played a part in their 1989-90 Fourth Division title triumph. After a stint at County, he was re-united with Cooper at Birmingham City. After a spell at Bristol City, Dryden was recommended to Southampton by Saints' chief scout – Terry Cooper. He was loaned out to Stoke City, Northampton Town and Swindon Town before he joined his final league club, Luton Town, in 2001.

WEDNESDAY 14TH JUNE 2006

Tony Pulis quit as Argyle manager to surprisingly rejoin former club Stoke City, although the Potteries outfit had gone through a change of ownership since his previous dismissal from the Britannia Stadium and were owned by Pulis's close friend Peter Coates. A Pilgrims' statement read: "Given Tony's obvious desire to return to Stoke, it would have been not only churlish to stand in his way, but also counter-productive to the needs of our club at this vital time of the year."

WEDNESDAY 15th JUNE 2005

Bobby Williamson made a double signing as midfielder Bojan Djordjic and defender Anthony Barness completed moves to Home Park. Djordjic, a Serbian-born Swedish national whose father played for Yugoslavia, had been released by Rangers after previously playing for Manchester United; Barness, who started his career with Charlton Athletic and played for Chelsea, had been released by Bolton Wanderers.

FRIDAY 16th JUNE 1893

Scottish winger Patsy Corcoran, who started out his career with Celtic, was born in Glasgow. Corcoran joined Argyle as they entered the Football League in 1920 and made a scoring debut in a Third Division (South) 5-0 home thrashing of Brighton & Hove Albion. He played his last game in a 2-2 draw with Exeter City at Home Park on Boxing Day 1925.

SUNDAY 16th JUNE 1907

Bernard Oxley, a forward who played for the Pilgrims in the 1935/36 season, was born, in Whitwell. Oxley arrived in Devon via Chesterfield and both Sheffield clubs but failed to score in any of his 15 games.

THURSDAY 17th JUNE 2004

Argyle chairman Paul Stapleton revealed that the signing of Scotland international striker Stevie Crawford was made possible by record season-ticket sales. Stapleton said: "Because the fans have shown that commitment, we can say to the manager 'We are committed to you and to increasing the size of the squad'."

FRIDAY 18th JUNE 1920

Winger Jackie Wharton, who had to wait six years before fulfilling his potential, was born in Bolton. Wharton was given his debut by the Pilgrims as an 18-year-old at the beginning of the 1938/39 campaign and made such an impact in his 11-game season that he was snapped up by Preston North End just before the outbreak of World War II. He finally made his PNE debut in 1946 and went on to play more than 250 games for Preston, Manchester City, Blackburn Rovers and Newport County. Jackie's son Terry played for Wolves, Bolton Wanderers, Crystal Palace and Walsall.

WEDNESDAY 19TH JUNE 1918

Inside-forward Jimmy Buist, who made his Argyle debut aged 30, was born in Falkirk. Buist played for Dundee and Raith Rovers before the Second World War but made only one appearance for the Pilgrims, in a 2-1 home Second Division defeat by West Bromwich Albion, when he was called into the team as a late replacement for the sick Bill Strauss. Neil Dougall made his debut in the same match.

TUESDAY 19TH JUNE 2007

Argyle hosted pop superstar George Michael in the second of two summer concerts at Home Park, following the success of Sir Elton John's gig three weeks earlier. The huge stage took up nearly all of the Mayflower enclosure and part of the pitch, and dwarfed the main grandstand.

TUESDAY 20TH JUNE 1916

Jim McColgan, another Pilgrim whose career was destroyed by the Second World War, was born. The Irishman made one league appearance for the Argyle first team, as a late replacement for Dave Thomas in a 1-0 Second Division defeat at Burnley in February 1939.

SUNDAY 21ST JUNE 1998

Former long-serving Argyle player Kevin Hodges was appointed as manager in succession to Mick Jones following the Pilgrims' relegation to the Third Division. After winding down his playing career at Torquay United, Hodges, along with fellow ex-Pilgrims Garry Nelson and Steve McCall, had successfully managed the Gulls to the Third Division Play-Off Final the previous season, when they lost 1-0 to Colchester United at Wembley. With his Argyle background, and success at Torquay on limited resources, he was an obvious target for chairman Dan McCauley.

THURSDAY 21ST JUNE 2007

Hasney Aljofree, a key player in the Pilgrims' 2003-04 Second Division title-winning side, left Argyle to join Swindon Town, and rejoin Paul Sturrock. In five years at Home Park, defender Aljofree made 127 appearances, scored five goals, and had his nose re-arranged by opposition forwards on countless occasions.

SUNDAY 22ND JUNE 1924

Percy Cherrett scored the only goal of the Pilgrims' 1-0 victory over Porteños, a Buenos Aires team: their first game in a five-week tour of South America during which they played nine matches against various sides. Manager Bob Jack's tour party, which had arrived in Buenos Aires on *RMSP Avon*, did not return to Home Park until August but the long hot summer had no adverse affect on the following season as the Pilgrims finished runners-up for the fourth successive time.

THURSDAY 22ND JUNE 1995

Neil Warnock was appointed as Argyle's 24th manager following the club's relegation to the Third Division the previous season, when three different men – Peter Shilton, Steve McCall and Russell Osman – had failed to keep the Greens up. A play-off specialist, Warnock got Argyle promoted in his only full season in charge of the Greens, going up on a memorable afternoon at Wembley where they beat Darlington 1-0 in the Play-Off Final. The following season, Warnock fell out with chairman Dan McCauley and was subsequently sacked.

WEDNESDAY 23RD JUNE 2004

Home Park season-ticket sales surpassed 10,000 for the first time in the club's history as fans showed a keenness to get a regular view of Championship football for the first time. "I don't believe there was a culture for Argyle fans buying season-tickets in the past," said Argyle vice-chairman Peter Jones.

SUNDAY 24TH JUNE 1951

Colin Sullivan, the fans' choice as Argyle left-back in the Pilgrims' Team of the Century, was born in Saltash, Cornwall. For almost 30 years Sullivan held the record as the youngest-ever player to wear the green, making his debut as a fresh-faced 16-year-old at Rotherham United in March 1968, lowering the mark established by fellow Cornishman Richard Reynolds some three years earlier. He was capped by England at under-23 international, and went on to make 256 appearances for Argyle, scoring seven goals, before joining Norwich City.

FRIDAY 25TH JUNE 1971

Martin Barlow, one of a small band of Pilgrims to have made more than 350 or more appearances for the club, was born in Barnstaple. Midfielder Barlow made his debut as a 17-year-old substitute in the 3-1 win over Oxford United in the final home Second Division game of the 1988/89 season – and played his final match in an Argyle shirt almost 12 years later. He was a key component of Neil Warnock's 1996 Wembley winners, claiming six man-of-the-match awards in the latter half of the Third Division campaign, and laid on the play-off semi-final winner for Paul Williams. But for a succession of injuries, 'Chopsy' – joint player of the year with Carlo Corazzin in 1997/98 – would have made more than 400 Argyle league appearances.

FRIDAY 26TH JUNE 1931

Welsh winger Malcolm Davies was born, in Aberdare. Davies joined the Pilgrims from Aberaman – a junior side which at the time acted as a feeder club to Argyle's reserves and senior teams. He made his debut in a Second Division match at West Ham United in February 1953. A regular in the Greens' line-up between 1954 and 1957, he made 84 appearances, scoring 15 goals, before returning to Welsh non-league football.

WEDNESDAY 27TH JUNE 1906

Defender Harry Roberts, Argyle's regular right-back for most of the 1930s, was born in Yorkshire. Roberts joined the Pilgrims in 1930 after spending six years with Leeds United. He was pretty much an ever-present for the next seven seasons, playing 257 games before leaving Argyle to join Bristol Rovers. He also scored 21 goals, mostly from penalties.

TUESDAY 27TH JUNE 1967

Defender Tony James was born, in Sheffield. James was signed for Argyle from Hereford United by Neil Warnock at the beginning of the post play-off victory 1996/97 Second Division season, and made his debut in a 2-0 victory at Watford. The former Leicester City man played 34 times in the campaign before being forced to quit with recurrent injuries.

WEDNESDAY 28TH JUNE 2006

Ian Holloway was appointed Argyle manager in succession to Tony Pulis. Holloway had been out of football since the previous February, when he was suspended by employers Queens Park Rangers after being linked to the managerial vacancy at Leicester City. Following this gardening leave, he settled up with QPR and took over at Home Park. After a successful 17 months, including taking the Pilgrims to only a second ever FA Cup quarter-final. With the club seventh in the Championship, Holloway resigned to take the manager's job at... Leicester City.

SUNDAY 29TH JUNE 1924

Argyle lost 3-0 to Argentinos in the second of their nine-game South American tour. *The Argyle Handbook* of 1954-55 records: "At the conclusion of the tour, Mr Bob Jack declared that the standard of South American football was higher than he had anticipated and was quite equal to Third Division standard at home." Six years later, Uruguay won the World Cup.

SUNDAY 29TH JUNE 1952

Barry Silkman, who played for 10 different clubs in 13 seasons, was born in Stepney. Argyle were club three in the career of Silkman, who moved to the Pilgrims from Crystal Palace by Malcolm Allison, and from the Pilgrims to Manchester City by the same man. He made 14 appearances in the Third Division Pilgrims' midfield of 1978/79, scoring twice. He subsequently became a well-known football agent.

FRIDAY 30TH JUNE 1972

Lee Power, who was, at various times in his career, a player, a director, a chairman, an agent, a manager, a racehorse owner and a sports publisher, was born in Lewisham. Forward Power, who played 16 league games for the Pilgrims in 1998, came to Devon after spells at Norwich City, Charlton Athletic, Sunderland, Portsmouth, Bradford City, Peterborough United, Dundee, Hibernian and Ayr United. A Republic of Ireland under-21 international, he made his debut at the beginning of the 1998/99 season but failed to settle, or score, and joined Halifax Town before the New Year.

PLYMOUTH ARGYLE
On This Day

JULY

THURSDAY 1st JULY 2004

Manager Bobby Williamson appointed fellow Scot Gerry McCabe, a former playing colleague and close friend for 25 years, to the Argyle coaching staff. "If anything bad happens to me, something worse happens to him – you need somebody about who is like that!" said Argyle boss Williamson.

SATURDAY 2nd JULY 1949

Brian Taylor, who spent one very successful year at Home Park in the late 1970s, was born in Gateshead. Taylor made his Argyle debut in October 1977 following a move from Walsall, for whom he had played more than 200 league games. Fifty weeks later, Taylor bowed out from Home Park after 35 Third Division games and five goals.

THURSDAY 3rd JULY 2003

Argyle midfielder Jason Bent was recalled to the Canada squad for the CONCACAF Gold Cup. Bent was an integral part of the Argyle team that won the 2001/02 Third Division title, and played 32 times for his country, including helping them to third place in the 2002 Gold Cup. He suffered a serious knee injury playing for Canada against the Republic of Ireland in November 2003 which, although he made a couple of cameo appearances for the Pilgrims towards the end of the 2003/04 Second Division championship-winning campaign, effectively ended his career.

FRIDAY 4th JULY 1924

Jack Smith scored twice as Argyle won for the second time on their post-season tour of South America, beating the Uruguay national team 4-0. Jimmy Logan and Jack Leslie were also on the scoresheet. Logan and Leslie were fixtures in the Argyle side throughout the 1920s, making nearly 700 appearances between them, and scoring 149 goals.

FRIDAY 4th JULY 2003

Defender Peter Gilbert joined the Pilgrims on a three-month loan from Birmingham City as Argyle returned to Home Park for pre-season training. Gilbert, whose father Tim had played for Sunderland, later earned a permanent deal and played 40 league games in the season's Second Division title success.

FRIDAY 5TH JULY 1935

Andy Nelson, who made 99 Argyle appearances between 1965 and 1968, was born in London. The centre-half stood out in the Ipswich Town team that had risen from the Third Division to win the Football League in 1961-62. He was signed by Derek Ufton from Leyton Orient and, after making his debut in a 2-1 Second Division defeat at home to Coventry City in October 1965, played at Home Park for three seasons before retiring after the 1967-68 campaign.

SUNDAY 6TH JULY 1924

In the fourth game of their South American tour, Argyle draw 0-0 with Rosarinos, a team based in the Argentinian city of Rosario. Other teams in the city include Rosario Central and Newell's Old Boys, a side named by ex-pupils of the English High School of Rosario in homage to its director and football coach, English immigrant Isaac Newell.

WEDNESDAY 6TH JULY 1988

Ken Brown was appointed Argyle manager in succession to Dave Smith, who had left to join his native Dundee. Brown arrived from Norwich City – via a one-match tenure at Shrewsbury Town – where he had twice gained promotion to the top-flight and won the League Cup. After two uneventful seasons, he was sacked with the team in the wrong half of the Second Division.

MONDAY 7TH JULY 2003

The Argyle Superstore opened for the first time. Situated by the club's offices at the bottom end of the Higher Home Park car-park, the building replaced the old club shop that had been adjacent to the main gates.

TUESDAY 8TH JULY 1924

Argyle lost 2-1 in the fifth game of their ground-breaking tour of South America. The Argyle goal was scored by defender Moses Russell, who had captured the imagination of the local media. One journalist wrote: "His effective style, precise judgment, accurate and timely clearances, powerful kicking, and no less useful work with his head… one of the most wonderful backs and one of the brainiest players ever seen on the football field."

FRIDAY 8TH JULY 1960

Goalkeeper Dave Philp was born, in Fowey, Cornwall. Philp played in local football for Newquay before he joined the Pilgrims in summer 1984. He conceded four on his home debut as Argyle beat Preston North End 6-4 and went on to make six more starts. He was among many understudies who found it impossible to upstage Geoff Crudgington.

WEDNESDAY 9TH JULY 1924

Despite having played only 24 hours previously, Argyle drew 1-1 with Boca Juniors on their South American tour. For the second game running, their scorer was Moses Russell, who equalised from the penalty spot with the last kick of an abandoned game. Supporters invaded the pitch after Boca scored, forcing the Argyle players to retreat to the dressing rooms. The match resumed after half an hour's delay, but a further invasion was sparked when referee Fred Reeve – a Plymothian who had travelled with the Greens – awarded a penalty against the home side. Cue another invasion and another retreat to the dressing-rooms, where it was decided that Patsy Corcoran would deliberately miss the spot-kick. On resuming, Corcoran placed the ball, but Russell shoved him aside and blasted it into the net. The Boca fans invaded the pitch again, and the match was abandoned.

WEDNESDAY 9TH JULY 1947

Alan Welsh, who hailed from Edinburgh, was born. Welsh was poached from Devon neighbours Torquay United by manager Ellis Stuttard in the summer of 1972, after 150-plus games for the Gulls on the wing. He was leading scorer in his first season, and pivotal to Argyle's League Cup success in the subsequent campaign. He played his last game for the Greens midway through their 1974-75 Third Division promotion season before joining AFC Bournemouth.

WEDNESDAY 10TH JULY 1912

Wilf Chitty was born in Walton-on-Thames. Chitty came to Home Park in December 1938 after scoring 16 goals in 45 games for Chelsea – but only played three times for the Pilgrims before moving to Reading.

SATURDAY 10TH JULY 2004

The Pilgrims won friendlies in two different parts of the Westcountry, simultaneously. A team coached by Gerry McCabe defeated city side Plymouth Parkway 3-0, while, at the same time, manager Bobby Williamson watched another line-up win 4-2 at St Blazey. David Friio, Lee Hodges and Stephen Milne scored against Parkway, with Marino Keith's hat-trick and Stevie Crawford accounting for St Blazey.

TUESDAY 11TH JULY 1967

Kenny Brown, Argyle's Player of the Year in 1990/91, was born in Upminster. The son of former West Ham stalwart Ken Brown, Kenny was signed by his father for the Pilgrims from Norwich City – where the pair had also been together – in 1988 and was a virtual ever-present at right-back for the next three Second Division seasons, outlasting his father by a year. It was in his final season that he picked up the fans' award before leaving for his father's alma mater at Upton Park.

MONDAY 11TH JULY 2005

Graham Coughlan, the Pilgrims' leading scorer in their 2001/02 Third Division title-winning campaign, left Home Park after four years to rejoin former manager Paul Sturrock at Sheffield Wednesday. 'Cocko', a central defender with an eye for goal, was also voted in to the 2001/02 PFA Third Division team of the year, as well as taking the Argyle fans' accolade as Player of the Season. Two seasons later, the Irishman was named the Second Division Player of the Season as the Pilgrims won the league title, and was also voted into the Argyle Team of the Century.

WEDNESDAY 12TH JULY 1944

Forward Danny Trainor was born, in Belfast. Trainor arrived at Home Park from Irish club Crusaders in the summer of 1968 with one full Northern Ireland cap and a big reputation in his home country. He made his debut in a 1-0 Third Division win against AFC Bournemouth, scoring three goals in seven games, before it became obvious he was not up to scratch. He returned home after one season to join Waterford.

WEDNESDAY 12TH JULY 2006

The Pilgrims won their first game under Ian Holloway, a 4-0 success at non-league Tiverton Town. A goal on the stroke of half-time from Luke Summerfield was added to by second-half strikes from Mathias Kouo-Doumbe, Chris Zebroski and Anthony Mason.

SUNDAY 13TH JULY 1924

Game seven of the Pilgrims' South American close-season tour saw Alf Rowe's goal give them a 1-0 win over Argentinos. It was a high point for Rowe, who failed to score for the Pilgrims back in England.

THURSDAY 13TH JULY 2006

Plymouth University student Josh Clapham was called into Argyle's first-team squad as cover for Luke McCormick. Clapham, who had been recommended to the club by ex-striker Fred Binney, was set to graduate in Politics & Business but missed the ceremony to go on a pre-season visit to Austria, swapping the British Universities League to face Real Madrid.

WEDNESDAY 14TH JULY 2004

A Home Park crowd of around 4,000 honoured former Argyle boss Dave Smith in a testimonial featuring two clubs that he managed. Argyle beat Torquay United 2-1 with goals from David Friio and David Norris.

FRIDAY 14TH JULY 2006

Argyle signed striker Sylvan Ebanks-Blake from Manchester United on a three-year deal for an initial £200,000. After 21 goals in 56 leagues games, Ebanks-Blake was transferred to Wolves for £1.5m.

SUNDAY 15TH JULY 2001

David Tall was named Argyle chief executive. A retired naval captain with 36 years experience, Tall took over from Roger Matthews. Previously he'd been chairman of the Royal Navy and Combined Services FA.

SATURDAY 15TH JULY 2006

Argyle warmed up for a pre-season tour of Austria with a 3-0 win over Grays Athletic. The Pilgrims gave a debut to Sylvan Ebanks-Blake but the newcomer was eclipsed by Nick Chadwick, who scored a hat-trick in his first game after recovering from Achilles troubles.

HASNEY ALJOFREE AND GUTI, ARGYLE V REAL MADRID: SEE 16th JULY 2006

FRIDAY 16TH JULY 2004

Argyle flew out from Birmingham to Austria to begin a 10-day, three-match, pre-season visit to Obertraun, where they had been based 12 months earlier. New manager Bobby Williamson's squad included summer signings Stevie Crawford, Mathias Kouo-Doumbe, Keith Lasley, Lee Makel and Steven Milne.

SUNDAY 16TH JULY 2006

The Pilgrims flew to Austria for a pre-season training camp that included a prestigous friendly against Real Madrid. The game was arranged after the Spaniards – who were late arranging their own pre-season after a club presidential election and managerial appointment of Fabio Capello – discovered Argyle had booked their favoured hotel. Real offered Argyle the chance to play them if they moved to an alternative training base.

SATURDAY 17TH JULY 2004

Argyle made a confident start to their pre-season tour of Austria with a 4-0 victory over SV Bad Aussee. Marino Keith scored twice to put the Pilgrims 2-0 ahead at half-time, substitute Steven Milne added the third, and Keith Lasley completed the scoring.

SUNDAY 17TH JULY 2005

Argyle set off at 7am from Plymouth for a 14-hour journey to reach their pre-season training camp in Holmsund, north-east Sweden. After a coach trip to London Heathrow, they flew to the Swedish capital Stockholm and then caught an internal flight to Umea, about 15 kilometres from Holmsund, finally arriving at the Vasterbacken Hotel and Conference Centre shortly after 9pm local time.

FRIDAY 18TH JULY 1924

The penultimate game of Argyle's tour of South America saw them draw 1-1 with the Uruguayan national team, thanks to a goal from Patsy Corcoran, a tall Scottish winger who played 198 games for the Greens.

SUNDAY 18TH JULY 1948

Former Middlesbrough midfielder Ray Lugg was born in Jarrow. Lugg joined Argyle in 1972, and made his debut in a 1-0 defeat at Rotherham on the opening day of the Third Division season.

TUESDAY 19th JULY 2005

Argyle posted a comfortable victory in the first match of their pre-season tour to Sweden, beating Betsele IF 9-0 with Ákos Buzsáky and Nick Chadwick scoring twice. Also on the mark was Estonian international striker Ingemar Teever, a trialist who had also scored for TVMK in a 1-1 draw at home to Finns MyPa in the Uefa Cup first qualifying round five days earlier. Bjarni Guðjónsson, Paul Wotton, Tony Capaldi and Luke Summerfield claimed the Pilgrims' other goals.

WEDNESDAY 19th JULY 2006

Argyle secured a 5-1 win over FC Gratkorn in the first fixture of their Austrian pre-season tour. The Pilgrims went a goal down to their Austrian second-tier opponents but hit back through Sylvan Ebanks-Blake's two first-half strikes. Reuben Reid and Dutch trialist Muhamadu Ebad scored after the break and defender Hasney Aljofree then thumped home a penalty.

SUNDAY 20th JULY 1924

Argyle lost the final game of their nine-game South American exhibition tour, 1-0 to Argentinos. The tour thus ended with three wins, three draws (one of which was in an abandoned match) and three defeats.

TUESDAY 20th JULY 2004

Bobby Williamson tasted defeat as Argyle manager for the first time when the Pilgrims lost 3-1 to SV Wacker Burghausen in the second game of their pre-season visit to Austria. The Greens won all three of their league matches at the end of the previous Championship campaign after Williamson was appointed and had beaten Torquay United and Austrian part-timers Bad Aussee in pre-season.

SATURDAY 21st JULY 1990

Argyle's first ever pre-season training camp abroad was instigated by David Kemp who had begun his managerial career in Sweden, to where he returned in his first summer in charge of the Pilgrims. The first match of the tour was at Tvaaker, a Fourth Division club, and Argyle won 3-2. Two goals from Adam King and another from David Byrne earned the victory.

SATURDAY 21st JULY 2001

Paul Sturrock's Argyle began their week-long pre-season tour of Scotland with a 1-0 win against Third Division Montrose. A goal from Kevin Wills, who scored with his first touch after coming on as a substitute for Sean Evers, settled the issue.

SUNDAY 21st JULY 2002

Goals from Ian Stonebridge, Michael Evans and Blair Sturrock gave Argyle a 3-2 victory over Scottish Second Division Brechin City in the first, delayed, game of their pre-season tour of Scotland.

FRIDAY 21st JULY 2006

Argyle were beaten 1-0 by Real Madrid in the second game of their Austrian tour. The Pilgrims went down to a 75th minute penalty from Brazilian striker Julio Cesar Baptista but were not disgraced in a prestigious friendly that was rarely an uneven contest. The game was watched by a crowd estimated at 1,500 spectators, which included 250 Argyle fans, and, although Real gave some of their Brazilian and Spanish World Cup players the game off, their side included Jonathan Woodgate, Thomas Gravesen, Ivan Helguera, Guti, Antonio Cassano and several other internationals.

MONDAY 22nd JULY 2002

Argyle's second game in two days on their pre-season trip to Scotland ended in a second successive victory as goals from Nathan Lowndes and Craig Taylor gave them a 2-1 win over Third Division Montrose.

SUNDAY 22nd JULY 2007

Argyle arrived in the Austrian spa resort of Loipersdorf for their pre-season tour of Austria after a dramatic flight from London Stansted. The Pilgrims' plane had to twice abort its landing at Graz Airport after being severely buffeted by high winds. It eventually touched down at Klagenfurt, 80 miles west of its intended landing.

MONDAY 23rd JULY 1990

The second match of Argyle's pre-season in Sweden against Third Division side IFK Trelleborg ended in a goalless draw. The small band of Pilgrims' fans who had made the trip complained less about the standard of football and more about the price of beer, which was about £6 a pint.

MONDAY 23RD JULY 2001

The Pilgrims' unbeaten start to their pre-season campaign came to an end when they lost 1-0 at East Fife's Bayview Stadium. James Allan scored the game's only goal direct from a 20-yard free-kick, whilst 34-year-old Republic of Ireland centre-back Alan Kernaghan lined up for the Greens. He never featured in an Argyle league game.

FRIDAY 23RD JULY 2004

Argyle suffered the second consecutive defeat of their pre-season tour to Austria when they lost 2-0 to Czech top-flight side České Budějovice.

SATURDAY 23RD JULY 2005

Argyle concluded their pre-season tour of Sweden with a one-sided 5-1 victory over hosts Holmsund, an amateur side that played in one of Sweden's 12 regionalised fourth-tier divisions. Tony Capaldi, Nick Chadwick, Scott Taylor (2) and Anthony Barness scored.

WEDNESDAY 24TH JULY 2002

Argyle continued the winning habit on tour in Scotland with a 1-0 win at Second Division Forfar, thanks to a first-half goal from Marino Keith.

TUESDAY 24TH JULY 2007

Argyle held Turkish top-flight team Gençlerbirliği to a 1-1 draw in the first of two friendlies on tour in Austria. After conceding an early goal, Plymouth equalised late on through substitute striker Reuben Reid.

WEDNESDAY 25TH JULY 1990

In the last match of the Pilgrims' pre-season visit to Sweden, Argyle got their best result of the trip, a 3-1 win at Second Division Lund. Barnstaple-born 19-year-old Owen Pickard scored all three goals to earn himself a place alongside Robbie Turner when the Second Division campaign opened at Newcastle United the following month, but he never established himself as a first-team regular, making only six starts in four seasons.

WEDNESDAY 25TH JULY 2001

Argyle comfortably beat Second Division Forfar 3-0 in the third game of their pre-season tour of Scotland at Station Park. David Friio, Ian Stonebridge and trialist Miguel Reisinho scored the goals.

FRIDAY 26TH JULY 2002

A 1-0 defeat by Clyde meant Argyle ended their previously unbeaten pre-season Scottish tour on a low. One bright spot against the Bully Wee was the emergence of 22-year-old French trialist Osvaldo Lopes, a midfielder who went on to play a part in the subsequent Second Division season.

SATURDAY 26TH JULY 2003

On the second leg of their pre-season Austrian tour, the Pilgrims drew 0-0 with Schwan Schwanenstedt and then lost 1-0 to Romania's Petrolul Astra Ploiesti in back-to-back games of 45 minutes each. The Blitz Tournier was played in heat in excess of 90 degrees.

MONDAY 27TH JULY 1896

John Youngman Thomson was born, in Greenock, Scotland. Thomson earned a move to Home Park in 1926 after impressing manager Bob Jack playing for Brentford against the Pilgrims the previous season. He made his debut in a Third Division (South) 1-1 draw with Crystal Palace at Home Park and held his place for six more games, when Fred Craig regained the goalkeeper's jersey.

FRIDAY 27TH JULY 2007

Argyle ended a two-match trip to Austria with a satisfactory 1-1 draw against top-flight Israeli outfit Hapoel Tel Aviv in the Dietersdorf Waldstadion. The Pilgrims conceded an early goal, but merited the second-half leveller from Hungarian midfielder Ákos Buzsáky.

SATURDAY 28TH JULY 2001

The Pilgrims concluded a week-long stay in Scotland with a 2-1 win against part-timers Albion Rovers, thanks to two goals inside four minutes from centre-backs Mick Heathcote and Graham Coughlan.

SUNDAY 28TH JULY 2002

A fluke goal from winger David Beresford saved Argyle from an embarrassing defeat by local part-timers Bad Ischl on the final game of their winless pre-season visit to Austria. An attempted clearance from a defender hit Beresford on the shins and bounced into the net to secure a 1-1 draw against Bad Ischl, who played four divisions below the top-flight of Austrian football.

MONDAY 29TH JULY 1940

Johnny Brown, a player who made his debut in 1960 when Wilf Carter created an Argyle record by scoring five goals against Charlton Athletic, was born in St Kew Cornwall. The former Wadebridge inside-forward – known as 'Farmer' because of his rural roots – played only eight more Second Division games for the Pilgrims, scoring two goals.

SATURDAY 29TH JULY 1995

Neil Warnock's Argyle beat Truro City 6-0 in a pre-season friendly at the Cornwall Cup-holders' Treyew Road ground. The home side were managed by former Argyle captain Leigh Cooper but were no match for his old side, who won through goals from Wayne Burnett, Ronnie Maugé, Adrian Littlejohn (2), Michael Evans and Chris Twiddy.

WEDNESDAY 30TH JULY 1969

Argyle flew out to Dublin for a three-game pre-season tour of Republic of Ireland and drew 0-0 with Shelbourne on the day of their arrival. Billy Bingham's side included summer signings Winston Foster, Trevor Shepherd and Don Hutchins but were held by a young side of inexperienced part-timers at Tolka Park.

SATURDAY 30TH JULY 1977

Argyle made their bow in the pre-season Anglo Scottish Cup, which ran from 1975 to 1980, by beating Bristol Rovers 1-0 in a group game at Eastville with a goal from Terry Austin.

SATURDAY 31ST JULY 2004

Argyle beat former manager Paul Sturrock's Southampton 3-1 in a pre-season friendly at Home Park with the goals coming from ex-Saints player Michael Evans, Graham Coughlan and Steve Milne. One player not involved was Ian Stonebridge, a veteran of the club's two title wins in 2002 and 2004, who joined Wycombe Wanderers the same day.

PLYMOUTH ARGYLE
On This Day

P·A·F·C

AUGUST

SATURDAY 1st AUGUST 1903

Frank Brettell became Argyle's first manager. The Liverpudlian was a superb administrator, starting out as player-secretary-manager of St Domingo, forerunners of Everton. He joined Bolton Wanderers as secretary in 1896 before becoming the first manager of Tottenham Hotspur the following year. A year later, he left to become Portsmouth's first manager and led Pompey to second place in their first season in the Southern League. Using his many contacts, he successfully launched Argyle into the Southern League.

WEDNESDAY 1st AUGUST 1906

Scot Bill Fullerton was named Argyle manager, an appointment that lasted one season after the board subsequently decided to run the team by management committee for the following three seasons.

MONDAY 1st AUGUST 1910

Bob Jack was appointed Argyle manager, beginning a 28-year reign in charge of the Pilgrims. Jack, who had been the Greens' first professional player, had a spell as Argyle player-manager in 1905/06, and, on his return, won the Southern League title in 1913 and took Argyle into the Football League in 1920. He died in 1943, aged 67, and his ashes were scattered over the Home Park pitch.

TUESDAY 1st AUGUST 1967

Steve Davey scored early and late as Argyle kicked off a three-game pre-season tour of Holland and West Germany with a 3-2 win over GVAV Groningen.

WEDNESDAY 2nd AUGUST 1967

Argyle captain Andy Nelson was sent off for the first time in his career ten minutes from the end of a 3-2 defeat by Wuppertal SV – the second match of Argyle's pre-season warm-up tour across Holland and West Germany. The game was heading for a 1-1 draw when the German side was awarded a penalty which manager Derek Ufton called "a diabolical decision". Having converted that, Wuppertal were awarded a second spot-kick when Nelson clashed with Horst Heese off the ball. There was still time for 10-man Argyle to net a consolation through Steve Davey.

SATURDAY 2ND AUGUST 1969

The bright spot of Argyle's disappointing pre-season visit to Ireland was a 2-1 victory over Limerick. New signing Trevor Shepherd opened for Billy Bingham's side, with Mike Bickle adding the second.

TUESDAY 3RD AUGUST 1965

Manager Derek Ufton and 15 Pilgrims headed to Dusseldorf for a three-match tour of West Germany. Vice-president Harry Deans and long-serving club trainer George Taylor were also in the tour party, which was augmented several days later by director Brian Williams and club secretary Graham Little.

SUNDAY 3RD AUGUST 1969

Argyle crashed to an 8-3 defeat by League of Ireland champions Waterford on the final game of their below-par visit to Ireland. The carnage began in the ninth minute, by which time Trevor Shepherd had put Argyle ahead, when Waterford netted the first of three goals in six minutes. By half-time, it was 5-2, with Norman Piper having netted Argyle's second. The two sides swapped goals at the beginning of the second period, with Argyle's coming from home defender Jim McGough. Two more late Waterford goals completed the embarrassing rout.

WEDNESDAY 4TH AUGUST 1965

Argyle drew 3-3 with Alemannia Aachen on the first game of their three-match tour of West Germany. Aachen were 2-0 up at half-time but Mike Trebilcock and Frank Lord brought matters level. Alfred Glenski then appeared to have sealed victory for the home side before Barrie Jones crossed for Lord to score a second equaliser.

SATURDAY 4TH AUGUST 1979

Argyle began their second and final tilt at the short-lived Anglo-Scottish Cup with a 1-0 defeat by Fulham at Craven Cottage. It was the penultimate year of the competition, which had not really excited the British football-supporting public despite every attempt being made to give it the status of a top-level tournament. To this end, Newcastle United were expelled from the 1976-77 tournament for playing a weakened team.

FRIDAY 5TH AUGUST 1960

Goalkeeper Steve Cherry – a Wembley winner with the Pilgrims and 1987/88 Player of the Year – was born in Nottingham. Cherry had two separate spells with Argyle, joining the club first in 1986 – two years after being the Derby County custodian who let Andy Rogers' corner go in over his head in the FA Cup quarter-final replay at the Baseball Ground. He left after 73 league appearances and was brought back to Home Park by Neil Warnock in February of the 1995/96 Third Division promotion season, and made 19 more appearances for the Greens, his final one coming in the Play-Off Final victory over Darlington.

SATURDAY 5TH AUGUST 1967

Argyle ended an eventful three-match pre-season tour of West Germany and Holland with a 3-1 victory over KSV Holstein in Kiel. The Pilgrims won through goals from Keith Etheridge, Norman Piper and Duncan Neale, a substitute for Mike Bickle who was taken to hospital with cartilage trouble and did not play again until mid-November.

SATURDAY 6TH AUGUST 1977

Terry Austin scored as Argyle drew 1-1 at home to Birmingham City in their second game of the pre-season Anglo Scottish Cup competition. Coincidentally, in the only other time the Pilgrims took part in the tournament – two years later – they were again in a group with Blues, who they again played at Home Park, and who they again drew 1-1 against, again on August 6! On that occasion, Brian Johnson was the goalscorer.

WEDNESDAY 6TH AUGUST 2005

Simon Walton became Argyle's most expensive signing when he joined the Pilgrims from Queens Park Rangers for what was described as "an undisclosed club record fee". Leeds-born Walton was 20 when he signed but had already played five times at Home Park with four different clubs, losing only once. The 6ft 2in midfielder had won twice when he visited with Leeds, drew when on loan to Ipswich from Charlton, and won while on loan to Hull from QPR as the Tigers reached the Premier League for the first time.

SATURDAY 7TH AUGUST 1965

Mike Trebilcock scored his second goal of Argyle's West German tour to give the Pilgrims a 1-0 over Eintracht Trier 05. The game celebrated the 60th anniversary of Trier, who staged a party after the match that featured a male voice choir and orchestra.

SATURDAY 7TH AUGUST 2004

Three players debuted as Argyle kicked off their Championship campaign against Millwall. Keith Lasley and Stevie Crawford started, while Steve Milne came on as substitute in the 0-0 draw against the previous season's FA Cup finalists.

SUNDAY 8TH AUGUST 1965

Argyle ended their three-match tour of West Germany unbeaten with a 2-0 win over Wormatia Worms. Cliff Jackson and Frank Lord – with his third goal of the trip – netted early goals.

FRIDAY 8TH AUGUST 2003

Argyle launched their Centenary Season – and celebrated famous fan Michael Foot's 90th birthday – with a party at Home Park. Foot, also a Pilgrims' director, was given a special present of a place in Paul Sturrock's squad. The veteran left-winger, former Labour Party leader and ex-MP for Plymouth Devonport, was allocated the squad number 90, and his registration was accepted by the Football League.

SATURDAY 9TH AUGUST 1969

Right-winger Trevor Shepherd made a scoring debut in a 2-1 defeat at Reading on the opening day of the 1969/70 season. Argyle signed Shepherd after he had come to their attention while at Torquay United on loan from Coventry. After moving to Home Park, Shepherd lasted one and half seasons, scoring four goals, before dropping out of the game.

TUESDAY 9TH AUGUST 1977

Argyle's participation in the first Anglo Scottish Cup ended when they lost 2-0 at home to Bristol City to finish third in Group B, failing to qualify for the quarter-finals. Nottingham Forest won the competition, beating Leyton Orient 5-1 over two legs to give Brian Clough his first silverware at the City Ground.

SATURDAY 10TH AUGUST 1968

The first day of the new season saw the second coming of Frank Lord. Forward Lord played 69 league games for the Pilgrims, scoring at the rate of a goal every three matches, between 1963-66 before a jaunt up country with Stockport County, Blackburn Rovers and Chesterfield. He returned to Home Park in 1967 and reprised his striking role – while combining coaching duties – playing nine times and scoring twice.

FRIDAY 10TH AUGUST 2001

A new era began for the Pilgrims on the eve of the Third Division season as Dan McCauley stepped down as chairman and majority shareholder, although he remained on the Argyle board as one of six directors with an equal shareholding. The chairmanship passed to Paul Stapleton, a director of the club since 1998, while fellow director Peter Jones also remained on board and three new members joined: former Labour Party leader Michael Foot, Phill Gill, and Nick Warren.

SATURDAY 11TH AUGUST 1973

Argyle lost 1-0 at home to Stoke City in the first round of the Watney Cup, the Pilgrims' only appearance in the short-lived pre-season tournament. The teams scoring the most goals in each of the four divisions were invited to take part, with Argyle having amassed 74 Third Division goals – three behind Bristol Rovers – the previous season. A crowd of 17,501 saw the top-flight Potters win with a goal from Geoff Hurst.

SATURDAY 11TH AUGUST 2007

Argyle kicked off the new season at the same place, and with the same result they had ended the previous one, by winning their Championship encounter at Hull City's KC Stadium. Goals from David Norris, Rory Fallon and substitute Sylvan Ebanks-Blake earned a 3-2 victory.

SATURDAY 12TH AUGUST 1995

Argyle played their first game in the lowest tier of English professional football, and lost 2-1 at Colchester. Eight players, Chris Billy, Nicky Hammond, Mick Heathcote, Doug Hodgson, Chris Leadbitter, Adrian Littlejohn, Ronnie Maugé and Paul Williams, made their debut, with Littlejohn scoring.

SATURDAY 12TH AUGUST 2006

A late goal by substitute Nick Chadwick gave Argyle only their second away win on Wearside as they came from behind to beat Sunderland 3-2 in a Championship game at the Stadium of Light. Daryl Murphy netted for the eventual champions in the first 30 seconds but the Pilgrims earned a half-time lead through David Norris and Barry Hayles. A Sunderland equaliser threatened to deprive the Pilgrims of three points but Chadwick decided otherwise. Seven of the victorious Argyle players had suffered a 5-1 humiliation in the same fixture the previous year.

SATURDAY 13TH AUGUST 1977

Goalkeeper Paul Barron saved a penalty but was beaten by two more as Argyle conceded three spot-kicks in a 2-2 League Cup first round draw against Exeter City at St James' Park. Referee Les Burden awarded the Grecians their first penalty – for handball by John Craven – which Lammie Robertson converted past Barron. Two goals from Mike Trusson put the Pilgrims ahead before Robertson equalised from 12 yards after a foul by Barron. The Argyle goalkeeper finally got the better of Robertson after yet another penalty award following a Craven foul.

FRIDAY 13TH AUGUST 2004

Bobby Williamson's birthday. A 1-0 Championship victory at Cardiff City in front of Sky TV's cameras took Argyle to top spot, albeit until the weekend round of matches were completed the following day. The goal that separated the two teams at Ninian Park came when Stevie Crawford's header deflected off Lee Bullock for an own goal.

THURSDAY 14TH AUGUST 1952

Forward John Sims, one of the few players to have represented all three of Devon's professional clubs, was born in Belper, Derbyshire. Sims was taken to Home Park in 1979, from Exeter City, by manager Bobby Saxton, having played under Saxton at St James's Park. He scored on his home debut in a 2-0 win over Swindon, and scored 48 goals in 182 appearances across four seasons, before moving on to Plainmoor.

SATURDAY 14TH AUGUST 1993

Mark Patterson made the first of his 134 league appearances for the Pilgrims as they got the 1993/94 Second Division season off to a losing start with a 3-2 home reverse to Stockport County. Leeds-born Patterson was brought to Home Park by former Derby County team-mate Peter Shilton and quickly established himself as the Pilgrims' regular right-back. At the beginning of the 1997/98 season, he transferred to Gillingham, where he played alongside ex-Argyle team-mate Mark Saunders.

SATURDAY 15TH AUGUST 1981

Argyle made an uninspiring debut in the Football League Group Cup, drawing 0-0 at home to AFC Bournemouth in front of a crowd of just 2,707. The competition was short-lived, taking place in 1981/82 and 1982/83 only. There were 32 participants in the pre-season part of the competition, split geographically into eight mini-leagues, with the winners going through to a knock-out stage, which was completed during the season.

MONDAY 15TH AUGUST 1983

Luke McCormick, Argyle's goalkeeper for most of the 2003/04 Second Division title-winning season was born, in Coventry. McCormick started the campaign as back-up to Romain Larrieu, but the Frenchman injured his knee in an early-season game at Brentford and McCormick took over, dispelling anxieties about his inexperience to help set a club-record seven clean sheets between 28th December, 2003 and 24th January, 2004.

FRIDAY 16TH AUGUST 1935

Johnny Williams, one of five Pilgrims to play in 400 or more league games for Argyle, was born in Bristol. He made his Second Division debut as an 18-year-old amateur in 1955 impressing immediately as a half-back who loved to get forward, as 55 career goals was to demonstrate. During his National Service, he played in an Army XI alongside Bobby Charlton, Cliff Jones and John White and held his own to attract the interest of the big clubs. That was blunted by Argyle's steep £40,000 valuation and so Williams became a virtual ever-present at Home Park.

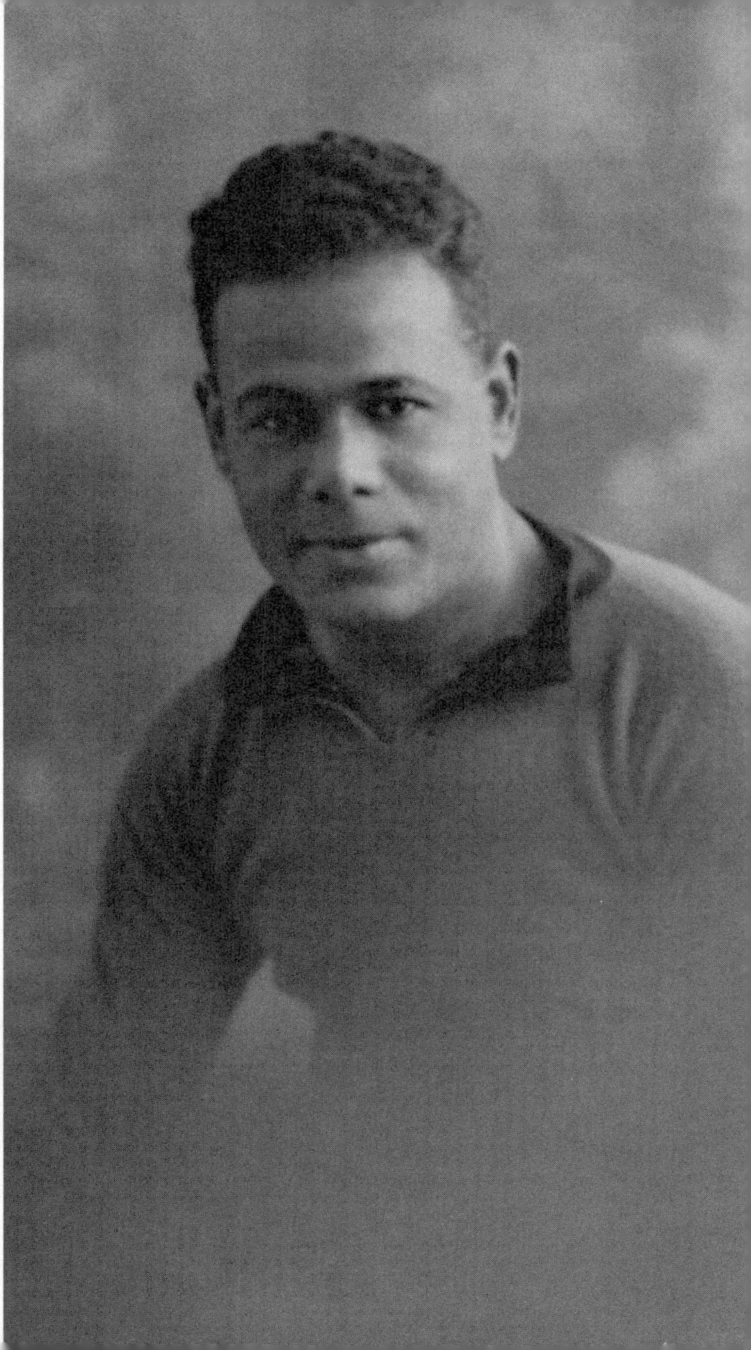

JACK LESLIE: SEE 17th AUGUST 1901

SATURDAY 16TH AUGUST 1980

Donal Murphy started his Argyle career with a bang, making a scoring debut on the opening-day 2-2 draw as the Pilgrims kicked off their Third Division campaign with a trip to Colchester United. The Dublin-born winger played for Torquay United in the previous two seasons, before his summer move along the south coast to Home Park, and was a virtual ever-present in his first season, chipping in with nine goals.

SATURDAY 17TH AUGUST 1901

Forward Jack Leslie, one of the Argyle legends, was born in Canning Town, London. His longevity –14 seasons as the club established itself as a Football League side – and his ability to regularly find the net means that Leslie places highly in both the club's all-time appearance list, and all-time goal-getters list. He played exactly 400 matches for Argyle, a total that has been bettered by only eight others: Kevin Hodges, Sammy Black, Fred Craig, Johnny Williams, John Hore, Pat Jones, Michael Evans and Paul Wotton. His 134 league and Cup goals is a figure topped only by Black, Wilf Carter and Tommy Tynan.

WEDNESDAY 17TH AUGUST 1977

Future club skipper and Argyle legend Paul Wotton was born in Plymouth. After suffering relegation to the Third Division as a 20-year-old, Wotton promised he would be part of the side that won back Argyle's place. He captained the Pilgrims to the Third Division title with a record 102 points in 2001/02, and was named in the Third Division team of the year. Two seasons later, he led the Pilgrims back to the second tier of English football. Reputed to have the hardest shot in the Championship, Argyle fans loved his fierce shooting from long-range, which, along with similarly ferocious penalties and free-kicks, brought him the majority of his 63 goals in 428 appearances for his hometown club. Both totals would have been higher but for a knee injury that sidelined him for 15 months in December 2006. Although he made a successful return towards the end of the 2007/08 season, his contract was not renewed, meaning the Pilgrims started the 2008/09 campaign without Wotton in the dressing-room for the first time in 14 seasons.

FRIDAY 18th AUGUST 2006

Argyle released young striker Chris Zebroski after a club disciplinary panel found him guilty of gross misconduct. The decision was taken after the panel considered an incident involving Zebroski and club captain Paul Wotton on a pre-season visit to Austria.

SATURDAY 18th AUGUST 2007

Boss Ian Holloway missed the 1-1 Championship draw with Ipswich Town at Home Park after being rushed to hospital two hours before kick-off… with a kidney stone. Assistants Tim Breacker and Des Bulpin took charge, as Sylvan Ebanks-Blake scored a late equaliser.

SATURDAY 19th AUGUST 1950

Eric Bryant scored both goals as Argyle won their first game back in Third Division (South) – 2-1 at home to Leyton Orient – following relegation after 20 years in the Second Division. It was the third game in succession that Bryant had netted. He never scored again.

WEDNESDAY 19th AUGUST 1981

Argyle's participation in their only Football League Group Cup ended with a 1-1 draw at Torquay United. David Kemp scored the goal. The previous day, Argyle lost 2-1 at Newport County, where John Sims netted. Two draws and a defeat saw them bow out of a tournament which was eventually won, the following April, by Grimsby Town.

SATURDAY 20th AUGUST 1955

Argyle lost 5-2 to Sheffield Wednesday on the opening day of the 1955/56 season. Left-winger Peter Anderson scored both of the Pilgrims' goals at Hillsborough against the eventual Second Division champions. Argyle were relegated.

SUNDAY 20th AUGUST 1961

John Clayton, a key component of Dave Smith's Second Division promotion side of 1985/86, was born in Elgin. The Scottish Schoolboy international joined Argyle from Tranmere Rovers in the summer of 1985. He had scored 36 goals the previous season for Rovers, as the country's top scorer. Clayton hit 11 goals in 36 as the Greens went up, before a short spell in Holland, and an even shorter one with Burnley.

SATURDAY 21st AUGUST 1948

George Taylor debuted at Barnsley as Argyle kicked off the new Second Division season with a 0-0 draw. Immaculate on and off the field, Taylor came to Argyle from Aberdeen, where he won the Scottish Cup. He played for the Pilgrims for two seasons, but remained at Home Park for the best part of 20 years as trainer, and even, briefly, as joint-manager with Neil Dougall.

SATURDAY 21st AUGUST 1965

Argyle were caught short at Portsmouth where they lost the Second Division Battle of the Ports opening-day encounter 4-1. John Hore had been inked in as the Pilgrims' first substitute, following new Football League regulations, but was called into the team after John Newman went down with a septic throat on the morning of the match. With no other cover, Argyle were unable to name a substitute and paid the penalty within ten minutes of kick-off when Doug Baird was injured and became a passenger for the rest of the game.

MONDAY 22nd AUGUST 1949

Inside-forward George Willis made his debut in a 4-1 Second Division defeat to Tottenham Hotspur at White Hart Lane. Former miner Willis spent seven seasons at Home Park.

WEDNESDAY 22nd AUGUST 1962

Wilf Carter, Micky Lill and Jimmy McAnearney all scored twice as Argyle beat Preston 7-1 in a Second Division game at Home Park. The Pilgrims' seventh, from McAnearney, was disputed by Preston goalkeeper Alan Kelly, who protested that the ball entered the goal through a hole in the side-netting.

TUESDAY 22nd AUGUST 2006

Championship Argyle were knocked out of the League Cup by League Two Walsall in a 1-0 first round defeat at Home Park. "If it was a boxing match, it would have been stopped," said manager Ian Holloway, after Saddlers' substitute Scott Dann delivered the knockout blow. Coincidentally, the scorer shared his name with another Plymouth sporting hero, the British middleweight champion boxer.

SATURDAY 23RD AUGUST 1947

Argyle lost 6-1 at Newcastle United on the opening day of the 1947/48 Second Division season in front of 52,642 fans at St James's Park, the largest league crowd that the Pilgrims have ever played before. Maurice Tadman scored the Pilgrims' goal.

SATURDAY 23RD AUGUST 1958

Argyle drew 1-1 against Hull City at Boothferry Park in their first game in the new amalgamated Third Division. Jimmy Gauld scored.

TUESDAY 23RD AUGUST 2005

Argyle won a Football League Cup tie for the first time in 13 seasons when they beat Peterborough United 2-1 in a first round match at Home Park. Scott Taylor scored the deciding goal.

TUESDAY 24TH AUGUST 1982

Joe Broad, a squad member in the Pilgrims' 2001/02 Third Division title success, was born in Bristol. Broad made one start and six substitute appearances during the Pilgrims' final stay in the basement division.

TUESDAY 24TH AUGUST 2004

Steve Crawford scored a bizarre goal as the Pilgrims went down 3-2 in extra-time to Yeovil Town in a Carling Cup first round giant-killing. Lee Johnson opened the scoring when he inadvertently knocked the ball past keeper Luke McCormick. He had been sportingly attempting to return it following treatment to injured Argyle defender Graham Coughlan. Yeovil manager Gary Johnson instructed his players to immediately allow Argyle to equalise, so the Glovers' 11 players stood back as Crawford received the ball from the re-start and scored unimpeded. Johnson netted twice more to give Yeovil one of their less-famous cup scalps.

SATURDAY 25TH AUGUST 1945

Argyle's first game after the Second World War saw them draw 5-5 at Southampton in a Football League South fixture. Paddy Brown scored a hat-trick for the Pilgrims, who led only once – at 2-1 – in the whole game. Dave Thomas netted the other two for Argyle, who went on to finish bottom of the Football League South, which was won by Birmingham City.

SATURDAY 25TH AUGUST 1956

Argyle were beaten 6-0 by Reading in a Third Division game at Home Park, their heaviest home defeat. It was the third of five successive losses with which the Pilgrims kicked off the 1956/57 season; a run which saw them concede 19 goals, following relegation the previous campaign.

SATURDAY 26TH AUGUST 1933

Sammy Black and debutant Jimmy Cookson scored two apiece as Argyle opened the 1933/34 campaign with a 4-0 home win over Manchester United. Cookson went on to score 37 goals in 46 appearances.

SATURDAY 26TH AUGUST 1995

Argyle lost their Third Division game at Chester City 3-1, a fifth successive defeat for new manager Neil Warnock, who made it six of the worst at home to Hereford three days later, completing a blank August for the Pilgrims: P6; W0, D0 L6; F3, A11. Warnock transformed the Greens into promotion-winners by the end of the campaign.

SATURDAY 27TH AUGUST 1921

Frank Richardson scored the Pilgrims' first Football League hat-trick on his debut as Argyle kicked off the 1921/22 Third Division (South) season with a 3-1 win at Bristol Rovers. Argyle finished the campaign level on 61 points with Southampton but lost out on promotion because of an inferior goal-average.

SATURDAY 27TH AUGUST 1927

Freddy Forbes became the third of only 10 Pilgrims to score four times in a Football League game when Argyle beat Merthyr Town 5-0 at Home Park on the opening day of the 1927/28 Third Division (South) season.

MONDAY 27TH AUGUST 2001

Underdogs at the home of the Football League's newest members Rushden & Diamonds, the Pilgrims, having failed to win any of their previous four games, came back from 2-0 down to level the game through goals by Michael Evans and Graham Coughlan. A phenomenal save by goalkeeper Romain Larrieu from Mark Peters preserved parity and Brian McGlinchey popped up with a late winner that began a club-record 19 matches undefeated in one season.

SATURDAY 28th AUGUST 1920

Argyle drew 1-1 with Norwich in their first-ever Football League game in front of 17,356 at Home Park. Summer signing from Bannock Juniors Jimmy Heeps – the only player in Argyle's 11 who had not been through the Southern League years – scored the Pilgrims' first league goal.

SATURDAY 28th AUGUST 2004

Bobby Williamson suffered his first league defeat as Argyle manager, four months after taking over from Paul Sturrock. Appointed the previous April a few days before the Pilgrims won the Second Division title, Williamson oversaw three consecutive league victories at the end of the 2003/04 campaign. The Pilgrims opened 2004/05 with a draw and three wins in the league before losing 3-1 at Watford.

SATURDAY 29th AUGUST 1925

Jack Cock hit the first of his four Argyle career hat-tricks as the Pilgrims won their opening-day Third Division (South) game against Southend United 6-2 at Home Park.

WEDNESDAY 29th AUGUST 1934

Jack Vidler hit a midweek hat-trick as Argyle beat Hull City 6-4 in a Second Division Home Park humdinger. Vidler scored 103 goals in 257 matches, making him the sixth all-time top-scorer in the club's history.

SATURDAY 29th AUGUST 1987

Argyle beat Reading 1-0 in a Second Division game at Elm Park to go top of the table... although it took time for manager Dave Smith to realise it. Smith missed the game's only goal – an oggie from Reading's Gary Peters a minute before half-time – because he had popped to the dressing-room to prepare his team-talk, and he watched the entire second half in the belief that the match was still goalless. It was not until after the final whistle, following a bizarre conversation with assistant Martin Harvey, that it dawned on 'the Ciderman' that Argyle had won.

SATURDAY 30th AUGUST 1919

Argyle resumed action after the First World War with a 3-0 victory over Swindon Town in a Southern League fixture at Home Park. Arthur Dixon scored twice.

SATURDAY 30TH AUGUST 1930

Argyle's first game in the Second Division ended in a 3-2 home defeat by Everton in front of 34,236 at Home Park. The Toffees had been relegated the previous season and were promoted back to the top-flight the following spring, by which time they had inflicted a 9-1 defeat on Argyle at Goodison and knocked the Pilgrims out of the FA Cup. Tommy Grozier scored Argyle's first Second Division goal.

SATURDAY 30TH AUGUST 1947

Argyle lost 3-0 at home to Birmingham City in Second Division to set a new club record of nine consecutive defeats – a string which was equalled in 1963. The Pilgrims broke the sequence before it ran into double-figures by drawing 0-0 in the return with Leicester City.

WEDNESDAY 31ST AUGUST 1927

Argyle beat Bristol Rovers 4-1 in a Third Division (South) game at Home Park, with Frank Sloan claiming a hat-trick. It was the second of inside-forward Sloan's two hat-tricks for the Pilgrims.

WEDNESDAY 31ST AUGUST 1938

Bill Hullett scored all three goals as Argyle beat Nottingham Forest 3-0 in their opening Second Division home game of the 1938/39 season. Hullett had been the Pilgrims' leading scorer the previous season – with ten goals from 11 games – and headed the charts a year later, with ten from 18, to earn himself a move to Manchester United.

SATURDAY 31ST AUGUST 1946

League football resumed after the Second World War with Argyle competing in the Second Division, having won only three of their games in the previous season's interim Football League South competition. It was a surprise, therefore, that they managed to beat West Ham United 3-1, especially since the Hammers nailed the first goal. Billy Strauss scored twice.

TUESDAY 31ST AUGUST 1965

An asterisk appeared on an Argyle team page for the first time when John Hore made the first of his 400-plus appearances as a substitute in a 1-1 Second Division draw at Charlton Athletic. He replaced Frank Lord.

PLYMOUTH ARGYLE
On This Day

SEPTEMBER

TUESDAY 1st SEPTEMBER 1903

Argyle played their first game as a professional club in a Western League game at West Ham United. They won 1-0, with Jack Peddie scoring the Pilgrims' first professional goal in front of around 4,000 people. The Argyle line-up was: Robinson, Fitchett, Clark, Leech, Goodall, Digweed, Dalrymple, Anderson, Peddie, Picken, Jack.

WEDNESDAY 1st SEPTEMBER 1948

Former player Jimmy Rae was appointed Argyle manager. Scotsman Rae had been assistant to previous manager Jack Tresadern, and he inspired the Jumbo Chisholm-led team to promotion from the Second Division in 1952 – as champions – although most of his tenure was spent trying to avoid relegation. As a player, Rae made 246 appearances in seven seasons and was the forerunner of David Kemp and Steve McCall in serving the club as player, coach and manager.

SATURDAY 2nd SEPTEMBER 1939

A goal by Welsh international Pat Glover gave Argyle a 1-0 Second Division victory at Sheffield Wednesday in the Pilgrims' last game before the Football League was abandoned because of World War II. It was Glover's third and last appearance for the Greens as he did not play again when hostilities ceased.

SATURDAY 2nd SEPTEMBER 1972

Brentford claimed a 1-0 Third Division victory at Home Park, despite protestations that Alan Murray's goal was a shot that missed. "The ball struck the side-netting and rolled over the top," claimed Pilgrims' goalkeeper Peta Bala'c. "Even the fella who scored was staggered when the referee signalled for a goal."

WEDNESDAY 2nd SEPTEMBER 1981

The first leg of Argyle's League Cup first round tie at Chester City was abandoned at 2-2 after a goal collapsed. David Kemp and John Sims scored for the Pilgrims when, with 12 minutes to go, Chester goalkeeper Glenville Millington collided with a goalpost in attempting to keep out another Kemp effort. The post snapped and could not be repaired, so the game had to be replayed the following Monday. It ended 1-1 and Argyle won the home leg 1-0.

SATURDAY 3RD SEPTEMBER 1938

Teenage winger Jackie Wharton made a sensational debut, scoring both goals in the Pilgrims' Second Division game against West Bromwich Albion at Home Park. Barely had manager Jack Tresadern's pre-match appeal for the crowd to go easy on the youngster faded away when Wharton scored. Although Albion levelled midway through the first half, 18-year-old Wharton notched the winner on the hour.

MONDAY 4TH SEPTEMBER 1905

Argyle drew 0-0 in a Southern League fixture at Luton Town, who were using Kenilworth Road for the first time. Argyle played, naturally, in green; the referee was a Mr Green; the Luton secretary was also a Mr Green; and, because it was the ground's debut, a ceremonial kick-off was performed by a representative of the local Greene King brewery!

WEDNESDAY 4TH SEPTEMBER 1957

Neil Langman scored the final of his four hat-tricks for the Greens when Argyle won 3-1 away at Reading in a Third Division (South) match.

SATURDAY 5TH SEPTEMBER 1903

Argyle played their first match in the Southern League, winning 2-0 against Northampton Town at Home Park. Jack Peddie scored the opening goal and John Picken netted the second. The full Argyle line-up was: Robinson, Fitchett, Clark, Leech, Goodall, Digweed, Dalrymple, Anderson, Peddie, Picken, Jack. The attendance was 4,438 and gate receipts were £124.

SATURDAY 5TH SEPTEMBER 1936

Jackie Smith scored a Home Park hat-trick as Argyle overcame Doncaster Rovers 7-0 in a one-sided Second Division game. Jack Vidler netted a couple of goals, with Sammy Black and winger Jimmy Hunter also on target.

SATURDAY 6TH SEPTEMBER 1924

Patsy Corcoran, Jack Leslie and Bert Batten each scored a double as the Pilgrims whipped Brentford 7-1 in a Third Division (South) game at Home Park. Corcoran had a benefit game two years later, with the opposition being provided by an Everton side that included Batten.

SATURDAY 6TH SEPTEMBER 1980

David Kemp scored the only hat-trick of his prolific Argyle career as the Pilgrims made light of being reduced to ten men for more than an hour to beat Carlisle United 4-1 in a Third Division game at Home Park. Pilgrims' midfielder Forbes Phillipson-Masters was shown the red card for tripping future England International forward Peter Beardsley with the score at 1-1, but Kemp ensured his former club were well beaten.

TUESDAY 6TH SEPTEMBER 2005

Bobby Williamson was sacked as Argyle manager after 17 months. His dismissal came during a reserve game at Home Park in which loan striker Matt Derbyshire, from Blackburn Rovers, scored a hat-trick against Swansea City. A statement issued at full-time noted that: "The board of Plymouth Argyle today announced it has served notice to terminate the contract of employment of Bobby Williamson."

THURSDAY 7TH SEPTEMBER 1911

Jack Connor, who scored twice for the Pilgrims on his debut against Nottingham Forest in 1936, was born in Garngad, Glasgow. Connor netted his double less than three weeks after his 25th birthday and went on to finish top scorer that season, with 17 goals.

SATURDAY 7TH SEPTEMBER 1974

Billy Rafferty notched his only Argyle hat-trick when he scored three-quarters of the goals in the 4-1 beating of Tranmere Rovers during the Dream 1974/75 Season. His partner in goals, Paul Mariner, was also on the scoresheet.

SUNDAY 8TH SEPTEMBER 1946

Mike Green, the most appropriately-named player in Argyle history, was born in Carlisle, Cumbria. Green joined the Greens in the summer of 1974 after winning promotion to the Third Division with Bristol Rovers and immediately repeated the trick as captain and was an ever-present throughout the entire league and Cup campaign in the heart of the Pilgrims' defence. After two and a half seasons in which he barely missed a minute, he left to become player-manager of Torquay United.

FRIDAY 8TH SEPTEMBER 1961

Former schoolboy international Nicky Law was born in Greenwich. The defender joined the Pilgrims from Blackpool in March 1987 – playing 38 league games, scoring five – before leaving for Notts County. He later managed Chesterfield, winning them promotion to the Second Division in 2000/01 despite a nine-point deduction following a Football League inquiry into financial irregularities.

SATURDAY 9TH SEPTEMBER 1905

Freddie Buck became the first Pilgrim to score four in a game (after the club turned pro) in a 4-1 Southern League win at Northampton Town.

SATURDAY 9TH SEPTEMBER 1995

Neil Warnock achieved his first home point as Argyle manager in his third Third Division game. Michael Evans' third goal of the season earned the Pilgrims a 1-1 draw against Leyton Orient and the point was enough to take the Greens off the bottom of the basement division for the first time since the start of the season.

WEDNESDAY 10TH SEPTEMBER 1930

The Pilgrims registered their first victory in the second tier of the English game at the fourth attempt when they beat Barnsley 4-0 at Home Park. Having already lost their opening home game to Everton – and losing at Bristol City and Bury – two goals from Sammy Black and strikes from Tommy Grozier and Alf Matthews gave them the winning feeling.

SATURDAY 10TH SEPTEMBER 1938

Argyle winger Jackie Hunter got the bird at Norwich City, where the Pilgrims suffered a 2-1 defeat in the Second Division. Hunter found himself through on goal early in the game when he tripped over a pigeon in the home side's penalty area. Bill Hullett overcame all opponents, feathered or otherwise, to score Argyle's goal.

SATURDAY 10TH SEPTEMBER 1966

Seventeen-year-old forward Richard Reynolds netted a Second Division hat-trick as Argyle beat Millwall 3-1 at Home Park. Cornishman Reynolds made his Argyle debut as a 16-year-old; a breakthrough which saw him selected for England youth international honours.

SATURDAY 11TH SEPTEMBER 1920

Argyle spectacularly ended a run of four winless matches to register their first ever Football League victory by winning 5-1 against Newport County at Home Park. George Sheffield scored twice, and Tommy Gallogley, William Dixon and Harry Raymond also netted after three draws and a home defeat to Crystal Palace.

SATURDAY 11TH SEPTEMBER 1965

Mike Trebilcock scored a hat-trick in a 6-1 Home Park thrashing of Birmingham City. By the end of the season, the diminutive Cornishman had left the Pilgrims for Everton, and enjoyed fleeting national fame when, after being preferred to England international Fred Pickering, he scored twice in the Toffees' 3-2 FA Cup Final win over Sheffield Wednesday.

TUESDAY 11TH SEPTEMBER 1973

Paul Mariner scored twice on his Football League debut as Argyle won a Third Division game against Rochdale 5-0, with fellow newcomer Alan Rogers scoring his first goal for the Pilgrims.

SATURDAY 12TH SEPTEMBER 1931

Jack Leslie scored a hat-trick in Argyle's 3-3 Second Division draw at home to Bradford City, the only time an Argyle player has scored a hat-trick at Home Park and not finished on the winning side.

SATURDAY 12TH SEPTEMBER 1959

The Greens suffered one of their heaviest home defeats when they were beaten 5-0 by Derby County in a Second Division game. It was one of only five Home Park reversals in the season, three of which were by teams that finished in the bottom six, like the Rams.

SATURDAY 13TH SEPTEMBER 1952

Three goals in six second-half minutes saw Argyle bounce back from 3-0 down to Rotherham United at half-time of their Second Division match at Home Park to win 4-3. Even though Arthur Smith scored for Argyle in the second half, the Millers led 3-1 with 22 minutes remaining. Two goals from Maurice Tadman quickly brought the game level before Smith fired home the winner.

TUESDAY 13TH SEPTEMBER 2005

Argyle, under caretaker manager Jocky Scott, avoided a club record when they drew 1-1 with Crewe Alexandra in the Championship at Home Park; the goal scored by Scott Taylor. They had already equalled their longest run of five games without a goal.

WEDNESDAY 14TH SEPTEMBER 1904

W Cox scored a hat-trick – only the second since Argyle had turned professional – in the 6-1 Western League thrashing of Brentford at Home Park. It was the first of four hat-tricks in a month by Argyle players, with Jack Picken grabbing two and Jasper McLuckie one.

TUESDAY 14TH SEPTEMBER 2004

The largest league crowd at Home Park since the ground was rebuilt in 2001/02 saw the Pilgrims surrender their year-long 22-match unbeaten home record, going down 1-0 to newly relegated Leeds United in a Championship game. The gate of 20,555 outdid the 19,888 that attended the previous season's Second Division title-decider against QPR.

SATURDAY 15TH SEPTEMBER 1979

David Kemp scored twice on his Argyle debut following a £75,000 move from Carlisle as the Pilgrims beat Wimbledon 3-0 at Home Park. Kemp was leading scorer in 1979/80 and 1980/81, and the supporters' Player of the Year in 1980/81.

WEDNESDAY 16TH SEPTEMBER 1953

Paul Barron, one of many Argyle goalkeepers to go on to better things after leaving the Pilgrims, was born in Woolwich. Barron spent one complete Second Division season at Home Park in 1977/78 before being snapped up by Arsenal. He was also the West Bromwich Albion goalkeeper that Tommy Tynan scored against when the Pilgrims knocked the Baggies out of the 1983/84 FA Cup.

SATURDAY 16TH SEPTEMBER 2006

Dutch defender Marcel Seip made his Argyle debut as substitute as the Greens lost 1-0 at Southampton in the Championship. The Pilgrims ended the first half with sub Paul Wotton at centre-back, and Seip at right-back, following injuries to Hasney Aljofree and Lee Hodges.

SATURDAY 17TH SEPTEMBER 1938

Bill Hullett scored the second hat-trick of his season in a 4-1 home Second Division victory over Luton Town. The Merseysider enjoyed a purple patch that saw him score nine times in the opening eight matches of the season.

SATURDAY 17TH SEPTEMBER 1960

George Kirby's hat-trick in the 5-1 Second Division win over Portsmouth at Home Park made him Mr Popular. Not least of all with Southampton, who paid £17,000 for the handsome Liverpudlian.

SATURDAY 17TH SEPTEMBER 1988

Another hat-trick on 17th September! Tommy Tynan hit three in a home Second Division 4-0 victory against Stoke City. He was helped by home debutant Calvin Plummer, who provided two of his goals.

SATURDAY 18TH SEPTEMBER 1926

Jack Cock hit the second of four Argyle hat-tricks – all in an 18-month spell – in a 4-0 home win over Watford in the Third Division (South).

MONDAY 18TH SEPTEMBER 1950

Born in Leeds, Ian Pearson, a teacher and part-time professional, enjoyed his first spell at Home Park between 1974 and 1976, when he made 12 appearances in the forward line after joining from non-league Goole Town. He was back in 1983/84, after more than 100 games for Millwall and Exeter City, for another eight appearances and one goal.

WEDNESDAY 19TH SEPTEMBER 1956

Defender Tyrone James, who played for Argyle between 1978 and 1982, was born in Paddington, London. James arrived from Fulham and played five seasons for the Pilgrims, racking up 90 appearances.

WEDNESDAY 19TH SEPTEMBER 1956

On the same day, tough-tackling Irish defender Gerry McElhinney was born in Derry. 'Rambo' was a regular member of Dave Smith's 1985/86 Third Division promotion-winning team after signing from Bolton Wanderers in January 1984 and had made just two appearances shy of his Pilgrims' century before moving to Peterborough United in 1988.

GEOFF CRUDINGTON & GORDON NISBET: SEE 22nd SEPTEMBER 1984

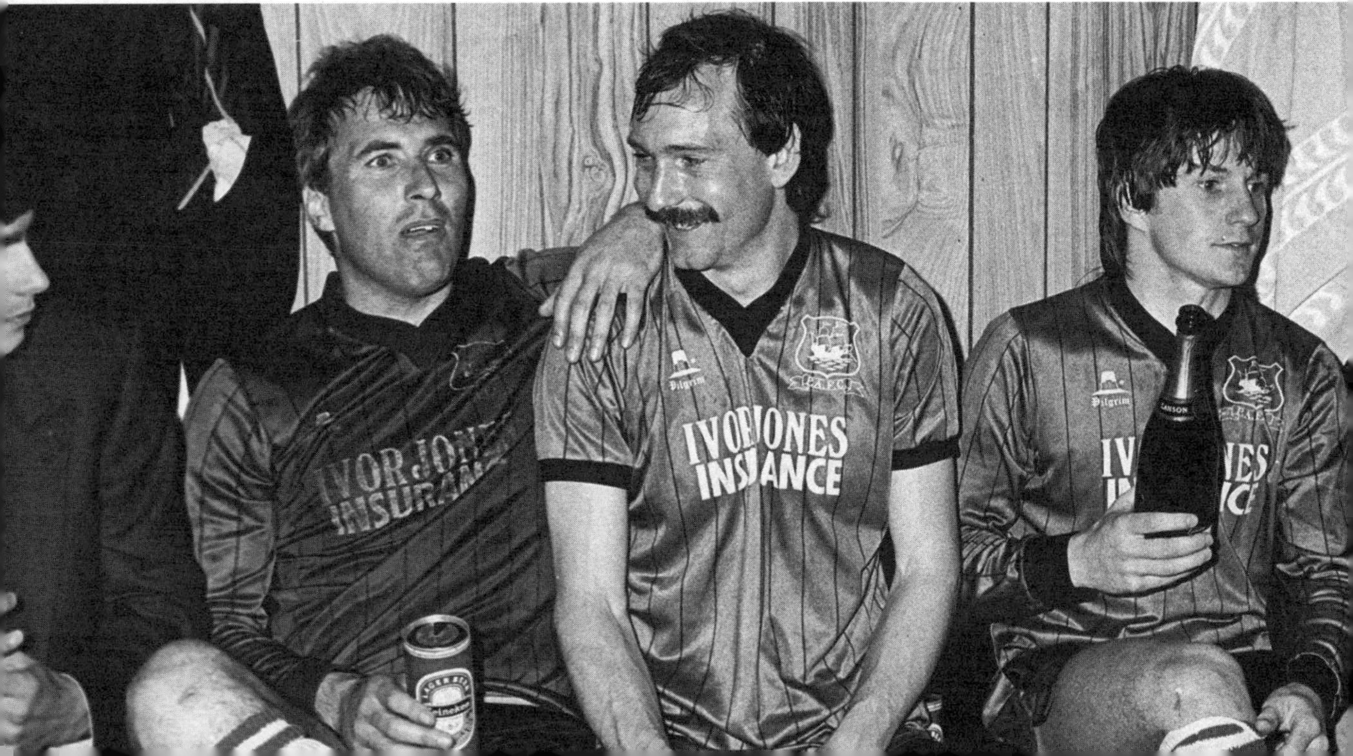

SATURDAY 20TH SEPTEMBER 1924

A Home Park hat-trick from Bert Batten helped Argyle to a 4-0 Third Division (South) win over Luton Town. Batten was snapped up by Everton the following summer after impressing on an FA tour to Australia.

FRIDAY 20TH SEPTEMBER 1968

Argyle overcame appalling weather and a 2-0 deficit to claim a 3-2 Third Division victory at Stockport County. In incessant driving rain, goals from Danny Trainor and Norman Piper pulled the Pilgrims level before Mike Bickle drove home the winner.

SATURDAY 21ST SEPTEMBER 1957

Winger Charlie Twissell, who represented Great Britain in the 1956 Olympics, made the final of his 42 Argyle appearances in a 1-0 Third Division (South) defeat at Gillingham. The Singapore-born speedster was discovered while playing in local Navy football and was still an amateur when he debuted for the Pilgrims' in 1955. He bought himself out of the Senior Service but remained an amateur to be eligible for the Melbourne Games. After Great Britain had been defeated 6-1 by Bulgaria in the quarter-finals, he turned professional.

SATURDAY 21ST SEPTEMBER 1963

Argyle had two players called Mark Smith, both defenders, on their books in the 1980s, though they missed playing in the same team by three seasons. Mark Smith, without a middle name, was born in Redruth in 1963 and was picked up by Argyle while playing with non-league Exmouth. He made three appearances before going on to play for Newcastle in Australia who were managed by former Home Park great Mike Trebilcock.

SATURDAY 22ND SEPTEMBER 1984

Argyle's defence produced an error-strewn performance to lose 7-2 at Bolton Wanderers in a Third Division game. Goalkeeper Geoff Crudgington started off with an air-shot fly-hack, and further mistakes from Kevin Hodges and Adrian Burrows allowed the bottom-of-the-table hosts to take control. At 5-2, Crudgington vacated his goal to play in attack after dislocating his finger, and replacement Gordon Nisbet, who had begun the game at right-back, was beaten twice more.

FRIDAY 22ND SEPTEMBER 2006

The way was paved for Argyle to take control of their own fate when the club and Plymouth City Council agreed a valuation of £2.7m for Home Park, allowing the club to begin the process of buying the ground.

WEDNESDAY 23RD SEPTEMBER 1964

Argyle embarked on their run to the semi-final of the League Cup when Malcolm Allison's Second Division side disposed of top-flight Sheffield United 2-1 at Home Park. Two goals from Frank Lord secured victory in the second round tie after Alan Birchenall had given the Blades an early lead.

SATURDAY 23RD SEPTEMBER 1978

Fred Binney scored a hat-trick at Hillsborough as Argyle ended Sheffield Wednesday's 15-match unbeaten Third Division run with a 3-2 win. After going 1-0 down, Binney scored twice to turn the game on its head. Ian Nimmo capitalised on an error from Argyle goalkeeper Martin Hodge – who later went on to play for Wednesday – to equalise but, three minutes later, Binney netted the 151st goal of his Football League career to notch a famous victory.

FRIDAY 23RD SEPTEMBER 2005

Tony Pulis was appointed manager of Argyle. Less than a day after his appointment, Pulis led the Pilgrims to a 0-0 Championship draw at Southampton. Having been sacked by Stoke City the previous June for "failing to exploit the foreign transfer market", he turned around a team that had been struggling to one that survived comfortably in 14th place in the Championship.

SATURDAY 24TH SEPTEMBER 1977

Former Liverpool midfielder Brian Hall scored the only goal of the game as Argyle won their Third Division match at Bradford City 1-0. University graduate Hall netted 16 goals in 55 games between 1976-77 after Argyle fans had helped stump up part of the £50,000 transfer fee through a 'Hall for Argyle' campaign. Hall, who also helped out in the club's commercial department, could not prevent Tony Waiters' side suffering relegation in his only full season.

FRIDAY 24TH SEPTEMBER 2004

Argyle defender Hasney Aljofree linked up with Paul Sturrock for the third – but not the last – time when he joined League One Sheffield Wednesday on loan. Aljofree first played for Sturrock, albeit briefly, at Dundee United, before joining him at Home Park. When Sturrock joined Swindon Town after being sacked by Wednesday, so did Aljofree.

THURSDAY 25TH SEPTEMBER 1980

Steve Adams, the midfielder who played in every one of Argyle's 52 league and Cup games in their 2001/02 Third Division title success, was born in Plymouth. Adams rose through the Pilgrims' ranks to debut in 1998 and went on to play 176 games, scoring seven goals. He was a vital member of the Second Division title-winning 2003/2004 team before joining former manager Paul Sturrock at Sheffield Wednesday.

SATURDAY 25TH SEPTEMBER 2004

Argyle lost their Championship encounter at Ipswich Town 3-2 after being 2-0 up within 13 minutes. It started to go wrong when Stevie Crawford doubled the Pilgrims' lead within 60 seconds of Steve Adams' opener. Tony Capaldi and Peter Gilbert went off injured before half-time, which destroyed Argyle's left-hand side, and Town took advantage to fight back and win the match.

SATURDAY 26TH SEPTEMBER 1925

Argyle came back from 2-0 down to thrash Aberdare Athletic 7-2 in a Third Division (South) game at Home Park. Jack Pullen and Freddy Forbes pulled Argyle level and Jack Cock ensured the Pilgrims led by half-time. Cock, again, Patsy Corcoran, Jack Leslie, and Sammy Black netted in the second half to complete the remarkable reversal of fortunes.

WEDNESDAY 26TH SEPTEMBER 2007

Argyle pushed Premier League West Ham United all the way before going out of the League Cup at Upton Park when Dean Ashton scored the Hammers' last-minute goal in a 1-0 third round victory. On the same date, at the same venue, 45 years earlier, the Pilgrims had lost 6-0 to the Hammers in the second round of the competition to record their heaviest League Cup defeat.

SATURDAY 27TH SEPTEMBER 1958

Despite two penalty misses from Wilf Carter, Argyle maintained their place at the top of Third Division with a 3-1 win over AFC Bournemouth at Home Park. Carter hit the bar with his first effort, and the post with his second, but goals from Neil Dougall, Reg Wyatt and Barrie Meyer achieved the victory.

SATURDAY 27TH SEPTEMBER 1980

John Sims and David Kemp gave Argyle a 2-0 Third Division win at Newport County as the Pilgrims achieved a ninth successive game without defeat – their longest unbeaten opening to a season since the Second World War. They managed another three games without losing.

TUESDAY 28TH SEPTEMBER 1954

Defender Mike McCartney was born in Musselburgh. McCartney was signed for Argyle from Southampton in 1981 by Bobby Moncur, who had managed the former Scottish Schoolboy international at Carlisle United, to where he returned after two seasons, 49 league appearances, and five goals.

WEDNESDAY 28TH SEPTEMBER 1966

The most maligned player in Argyle's history, Peter Swan, was born in Leeds. Swan was signed for Second Division Argyle in the summer of 1994 by Peter Shilton, having won promotion ahead of the Pilgrims with Port Vale the previous season. He scored for his new club on the opening day to put them 1-0 up against Brentford at Home Park but that was about as good as it got for the man dubbed 'the new Jack Charlton' at his first club, Leeds United. Argyle lost the game 5-1, and Swan and the Argyle supporters gradually became more and more mutually disenchanted as a poor season unfolded. One of the first things Neil Warnock did when he arrived the following season was to put Swan to flight.

SATURDAY 29TH SEPTEMBER 1906

Tom McKenzie scored a Southern League hat-trick in a 4-0 defeat of Reading at Home Park. It was the Pilgrims' third straight home victory of the season.

THURSDAY 29TH SEPTEMBER 1966

Fresh from winning the World Cup, an England team masquerading as a Football League XI beat the Irish League 12-0 at Home Park. Seven of the Boys of '66 started the game, although Jack Charlton, rather than team-mate Bobby Moore, was captain. Argyle defender Johnny Newman made an appearance, as did Jules Rimet.

SATURDAY 29TH SEPTEMBER 1984

A remarkable Third Division game at Home Park ended with Argyle beating Preston North End 6-4 for their first win of the season. Four goals were scored in the final five minutes, two from penalties, and Preston had two players dismissed. With PNE leading 3-1, manager Johnny Hore sent on on-loan striker Tommy English. The Leicester player helped set up Kevin Hodges and Russell Coughlin to bring the game level, but Preston, who had seen two-goal Jonathan Clark sent off, regained the lead through John Kelly's penalty. Immediately, English was brought down for Gordon Staniforth to equalise with another spot-kick. Preston's Tommy Booth was sent off for a foul from which Hodges put Argyle ahead before English completed the comeback.

WEDNESDAY 30TH SEPTEMBER 1908

Prolific striker Clarrie Bourton was born in Bristol. Bourton arrived at Home Park in October 1937 with a reputation as a goal-getter, having netted 173 times in 228 games for Coventry City. His stay with the Pilgrims comprised eight appearances in which he scored three goals.

SATURDAY 30TH SEPTEMBER 2006

Cherno Samba scored his only Argyle goal on his debut, eight minutes after coming on as a substitute, to secure a 1-0 Championship victory over Coventry City at the Ricoh Arena. Six years earlier, while a 14-year-old at Millwall, Samba scored 136 goals in 32 games to have Liverpool and Manchester United jostling for his services. However, the Lions rejected a £1.5m approach from Liverpool and Samba's career stagnated. Released by Millwall, he joined Argyle after a spell at Spanish side Cadiz but, after two starts, left the Pilgrims.

PLYMOUTH ARGYLE
On This Day

OCTOBER

SATURDAY 1st OCTOBER 1983

Coach Martin Harvey took temporary charge of Argyle following the resignation of Bobby Moncur as the Third Division Pilgrims lost 2-1 at Burnley. Harvey didn't help his prospects for the job on a permanent basis when Argyle lost a second league game under his charge the following week, by the same margin, at AFC Bournemouth – before giving way to John Hore. But he did inspire the Pilgrims to a League Cup draw with Arsenal in between

WEDNESDAY 1st OCTOBER 2003

Argyle manager Paul Sturrock mounted a vigorous defence of Peter Gilbert after his young defender had been abused by Home Park fans during a home defeat by Bristol City. "It's something I have never experienced in my life before, with any football club I've been at," said a furious Sturrock in his post-match press conference. "There was a cheer when he was substituted, which I think is absolutely disgraceful." Gilbert's response was to score two goals in four days, one in each of the Pilgrims' next two games, against Tranmere Rovers in the Second Division and Bristol City in the LDV Vans Trophy – the only two goals he scored in 84 senior appearances for Argyle.

SATURDAY 2nd OCTOBER 1920

In their fourth away game in the Football League, Argyle won away from home for the first time, beating Gillingham 1-0 in the Third Division thanks to a goal from Jack 'Ginger' Hill. The Pilgrims had softened up their opponents by beating them 3-1 at Home Park the previous week.

THURSDAY 2nd OCTOBER 1958

A second-half hat-trick from Peter Anderson saw Argyle come back from 4-2 down at half-time of their Third Division visit to Doncaster Rovers and earn a 6-4 victory. Argyle twice levelled in the first half, through Harry Penk and Barrie Meyer, but found themselves trailing by two goals at half-time. Two goals from Anderson brought the scores level before future Test-match umpire Meyer put Argyle ahead for the first time, leaving Anderson to ice the cake.

FRIDAY 3RD OCTOBER 1952

Mike Dowling, a Cornish midfielder, was born in Bodmin. Dowling played 35 games for the Pilgrims between 1970 and 1973 but left a mark far more indelible than some who have played many more games. Dowling, who was discovered playing for East Cornwall Schoolboys, scored two memorable goals against Brazilian club side Santos in a 1973 friendly, after a similar strike helped knock Yeovil Town out of the FA Cup the previous year.

SATURDAY 3RD OCTOBER 1959

Wilf Carter scored a hat-trick as Argyle beat Charlton Athletic 6-4 in a Second Division meeting at Home Park. A switchback encounter saw the two teams go in level at the break but the Pilgrims, whose other scorers were Billy Wright, Alex Govan, and Peter Anderson, forged ahead in the second 45 minutes. Charlton had their revenge later in the season when they won the reverse fixture 5-2 at the Valley.

TUESDAY 4TH OCTOBER 1983

Third Division Argyle banked record gate receipts of just over £45,000 for a Milk Cup tie which they drew 1-1 with First Division Arsenal in front of a crowd of nearly 21,000. Gordon Nisbet scored for the Pilgrims in the second round, first-leg encounter, with Graham Rix replying for the First Division Gunners who won the second leg at Highbury 1-0.

TUESDAY 4TH OCTOBER 2005

Paul Wotton, the most-successful captain in Argyle's history, led the Pilgrims in his testimonial game against Belgium side Anderlecht – an entertaining match which ended honours even in a 2-2 draw. The Pilgrims took a 2-0 lead inside the first 15 minutes when French central defender Mathias Kouo-Doumbe headed home Wotton's curling free-kick. Icelandic right-midfielder Bjarni Guðjónsson nodded in three minutes later. As well as leading Argyle to the Third Division title in 2001/02 and the Second Division championship two years later, Plymothian Wotton was the fans' Player of the Year in 2002/03 and 2004/05, and was the club's leading goalscorer in 2004/05 and 2005/06.

SATURDAY 5TH OCTOBER 1946

Scotsman Alex Govan made his debut in a 2-2 Second Division draw with Coventry City at Home Park. Govan was born in Glasgow and had two spells with the Pilgrims, scoring 30 goals in 117 appearances in his first Home Park stint, some of which helped the Greens to the Third Division (South) championship in 1951/52. He signed for Birmingham City in 1953, scored on his debut and played in the 1956 FA Cup Final with fellow ex-Pilgrim Gordon Astall. In 1958, he returned to Argyle and helped the Pilgrims win the Third Division championship before retiring the following year.

SATURDAY 5TH OCTOBER 1963

A 3-2 Second Division win at Home Park against Grimsby Town brought to an end a club-record 13 consecutive games without a victory. The sequence began with defeats at Luton Town and Cardiff City in the final two games of the 1962/63 season, and continued after the summer with six defeats and four draws before the Mariners' visit. Cliff Jackson, and Alan O'Neill scored the goals.

SUNDAY 6TH OCTOBER 1957

Bruce Grobbelaar, Argyle's goalkeeper in the 1996/97 Second Division season, was born in Durban, South Africa. After his medal-laden career with Liverpool, Grobbelaar made more appearances for the Pilgrims than for any other side. He was brought to Home Park by Neil Warnock the season after Argyle won promotion from the Third Division and helped them keep their heads above water despite the sacking of Warnock midway through the campaign. At times during the season, Grobbelaar only saw his team-mates on match-days as he successfully fought a match-fixing charge through the courts.

THURSDAY 6TH OCTOBER 2005

Argyle terminated the contract of Taribo West after a three-month spell at Home Park. The 42-times capped Nigerian defender, who was signed by Bobby Williamson the previous summer, had not featured in manager Tony Pulis's plans and looked unlikely to add to his five games in the green.

SATURDAY 7TH OCTOBER 1933

Eugene Melaniphy scored a hat-trick against Bradford PA as the Pilgrims won a Second Division game 4-1. It was the only hat-trick of his Argyle career.

MONDAY 7TH OCTOBER 1957

Kevin Bremner, who made five appearances for Argyle on loan from Colchester United, was born in Banff, Scotland. Bremner's solitary Pilgrims' goal, in a 3-0 win over Reading in February 1983, helped him to a unique record. Prior to playing at Home Park, Bremner – brother of Aston Villa European Cup-winner Des – had loan spells at Birmingham City and Wrexham, and immediately afterwards, he moved from Colchester United to Millwall. His first goal for Millwall meant that he had scored for five different Football League clubs in the same season.

SATURDAY 8TH OCTOBER 1904

Jack Picken scored the third hat-trick in Argyle's professional history, netting all three goals in a 3-2 Southern League win over Kent side New Brompton at Home Park. By the end of the season, Picken had moved to Manchester United, who he went on to lead to two League Championships and an FA Cup triumph.

SATURDAY 8TH OCTOBER 1932

Sammy Black scored a hat-trick as the Pilgrims beat Charlton Athletic 6-1 in a Second Division match at Home Park. Black is the all-time top scorer for the Pilgrims, with 185 goals, despite playing as a left-winger for the majority of his career. He was the only pre-Second World War player voted into the Argyle Team of the Century by the club's fans.

SATURDAY 9TH OCTOBER 1886

The Argyle Football Club played its first game, as part of the Argyle Athletic Club, against Dunheved College in Launceston and went down 2-0. The college was the alma mater of Frank Howard Grose and William Pethybridge, who had formed the club by inviting former pupils from local public schools to put together a team at a meeting in the Borough Arms Coffee Tavern, Bedford Street, in the centre of Plymouth.

TUESDAY 9th OCTOBER 1973

Argyle lit up the Winter of Discontent with their biggest League Cup win, a 4-0 second round win over Portsmouth at Home Park. Steve Davey netted twice, with Ernie Machin and Paul Mariner also scoring. Davey went on to claim a single-season club-record seven goals in the competition.

SATURDAY 10th OCTOBER 1936

The highest Home Park league crowd – 43,596 – saw the Pilgrims draw 2-2 with Aston Villa despite being forced to play more than an hour with only ten fully fit men after defender Harry Roberts became a passenger through injury. Argyle came from behind twice, with Sammy Black and John Connor scoring.

TUESDAY 10th OCTOBER 2006

Argyle manager Ian Holloway made an unexpected return to playing when, at the age of 43, he lined up for the Pilgrims' injury-hit reserves in a game at Liskeard's Lux Park. Holloway, who was 28 years older than some of his schoolboy team-mates, played the full 90 minutes as the Pilgrims lost the South Western League fixture 3-0.

WEDNESDAY 11th OCTOBER 1972

Tony Waiters was appointed Argyle manager in succession to Ellis Stuttard. The former goalkeeper won five England caps during a playing career with Blackpool and Burnley and made his name in management as the England youth team coach. He took Third Division Argyle to the League Cup semi-final in 1974 and, two years later, won promotion to the Second Division. After he left in 1977, with the club on the verge of relegation, Waiters moved to Canada where he rose to lead the Canadian national side.

SATURDAY 11th OCTOBER 2003

Six different Pilgrims were on the scoresheet as Argyle beat Tranmere Rovers 6-0 in a Second Division game at Home Park. David Friio and Paul Wotton started the ball rolling and, when full-back Peter Gilbert scored a rare goal on the stroke of half-time, the Greens sensed it was going to be a red-letter day. Second-half strikes from Marino Keith, Michael Evans and David Norris duly delivered.

WEDNESDAY 12TH OCTOBER 1904

Jasper McLuckie scored a hat-trick as Argyle beat Queens Park Rangers 3-0 in a Western League game. It was the second of three individual triples by Argyle players inside a fortnight, with fellow striker Jack Picken scoring hat-tricks either side of McLuckie's midweek magic.

SATURDAY 12TH OCTOBER 1935

Sammy Black scored a hat-trick as Argyle trounced Barnsley 7-1 on the Tykes' Second Division visit to Home Park. Jimmy Cookson chalked up a double, as did George Briggs, who netted 12 goals in 58 games for the Pilgrims.

WEDNESDAY 12TH OCTOBER 1960

Jimmy McAnearney and Cliff Jackson ensured smooth passage to the second round of the first Football League Cup as Argyle defeated Southport 2-0 at Home Park in front of more than 10,000 people. Although the Pilgrims reached only the fourth round of the competition, they played eight matches, needing replays to see off Torquay United and Birmingham City, and going out to Aston Villa after drawing the first match and suffering an abandonment in the second.

SATURDAY 12TH OCTOBER 1963

A 3-0 home Second Division defeat by Northampton Town sparked a club-record equaling run of nine successive losses that took the Pilgrims until mid-December to break. Unsurprisingly, the season was a struggle for the Greens, who avoided relegation by a goal-average just 0.04 better than that of Grimsby Town.

SATURDAY 12TH OCTOBER 1985

Two goals in the last four minutes from Garry Nelson dragged Argyle back from the edge of the abyss to secure a 2-2 draw at Walsall, who had previously not dropped a point at Fellows Park. All seemed lost when Mark Rees put the Saddlers 2-0 up in the Division Three game, and even Nelson's first goal, in the 86th minute, looked likely to be nothing more than a consolation. Nelson, though, squeezed an injury-time second past two-time Argyle goalkeeper Steve Cherry for an unlikely point.

WEDNESDAY 13TH OCTOBER 1920

Bill Shortt, who made 342 appearances in the Argyle goal between 1946 and 1956, was born in Wrexham. Shortt made his Football League debut for the Pilgrims in their first official game after the Second World War, having previously guested for the side while serving in the Army, with the permission of parent club Chester City. Following a £1,000 transfer, Shortt signed on full-time for a side that conceded 120 goals in the South West Regional League of 1945-46, following that with a 96-goal shelling in the subsequent Second Division season. Nevertheless, he was selected for the first of his 12 Wales caps in a Victory International against Northern Ireland, and stuck around at Home Park long enough to be part of the 1951-52 promotion-winning side.

SATURDAY 13TH OCTOBER 1923

Argyle beat Watford 1-0 in a Third Division (South) game at Home Park, thanks to a goal from Percy Cherrett. It was a case of déjà vu, as the previous week the same two teams had met at Vicarage Road, with the game ending in the same 1-0 scoreline, with the goal coming from the same scorer.

SUNDAY 13TH OCTOBER 1974

Scott Partridge – a player who had the honour of scoring both for and against Argyle in the same season – was born in Leicester. Partridge played seven games, netting two goals, for the Pilgrims while on loan from Bristol City in Neil Warnock's 1995/96 promotion season. When he scored in the home 4-2 win over Chester City on February 3, it was the second time he had made his mark at Home Park – having already notched on the same ground for Torquay United (on loan from Bristol City) in their 4-3 by Argyle defeat the previous October.

SATURDAY 14TH OCTOBER 1950

Maurice Tadman became only the eighth Argyle player to score four goals in a Football League game when the Pilgrims overwhelmed Aldershot 5-1 in a Third Division (South) game at Home Park. Tadman was the Pilgrims' leading goalscorer in five out of six seasons between 1948-49 and 1953-54.

SATURDAY 15TH OCTOBER 1932

Argyle pioneered air travel when directors and officials of the club flew privately to a Second Division game at Stoke City aboard a De Haviland Moth. Manager Robert Jack preferred his players to take a 16-hour round trip by rail. Stoke 2 Argyle 0; Directors 1 Manager 0.

SATURDAY 15TH OCTOBER 1966

Mike Bickle scored four times as Argyle thrashed Cardiff City 7-1 at Home Park. The Pilgrims netted 85 seconds into the Second Division encounter when Bluebirds goalkeeper Lyn Davies tripped Bickle to allow Norman Piper to net a penalty. It was not a happy week for Davies, who had conceded eight goals the previous Wednesday, playing for Wales under-23s against England at Wolves' Molineux ground.

SATURDAY 15TH OCTOBER 1983

Gordon Nisbet and Dave Phillips scored as Argyle gave John Hore a winning Third Division start as Plymouth manager, 2-1 at home to Oxford United. Cornishman Hore is one of only a handful of players to have played 400 games for the Pilgrims but his managerial career had less longevity. Despite taking the Third Division Greens to the semi-final of the FA Cup, he was sacked after little more than a year in the job. In his 60 games, he won 17, lost 27, and drew 16.

SATURDAY 16TH OCTOBER 1886

The second recorded result by a club bearing the name of 'Argyle' saw Frank H Grose and William Pethybridge's amateurs go down 2-0 to Caxton, a local Cornish side. Named after the Argyll and Sutherland Highlanders, an Army team based in Plymouth, their green-and-black kit was modeled on the Highlanders' tartan.

SATURDAY 16TH OCTOBER 1971

A Don Hutchins' double took Argyle to the top of the Third Division after they defeated Aston Villa 3-2 at Home Park. Hutchins opened the scoring and netted the Pilgrims' third, sandwiching a strike from Derek Rickard against the previous season's League Cup runners-up, for who Bruce Rioch and Geoff Vowden netted.

SATURDAY 17TH OCTOBER 1931

Jack Leslie scored four times as the Pilgrims trounced Nottingham Forest 5-1 in a Second Division game at Home Park. Leslie, who scored 131 Argyle goals, was one of the first non-white players to play professional football and was the victim of establishment racism. Having been selected to play for England, he had the invitation withdrawn because officials belatedly realised he was "a man of colour".

SATURDAY 17TH OCTOBER 1987

Argyle ended a run of ten Second Division games without a win when they beat Leeds United 6-3 at Home Park in a game missed by manager Dave Smith, who was up country, scouting. Argyle breezed into a 3-0 lead through John Clayton (2) and Kevin Summerfield, only for Bob Taylor and Glynn Snodin to reduce the arrears. Summerfield and Mark Smith made it 5-2 and Tommy Tynan completed the Greens' scoring.

SATURDAY 18TH OCTOBER 1958

Wilf Carter netted a hat-trick at Mansfield Town as the Pilgrims won 4-1 on their way to the Third Division title. Carter top-scored for the Pilgrims with 22 goals in the season as Argyle went on to win the first unified Third Division title, pipping Hull City by one point.

SATURDAY 18TH OCTOBER 2003

Argyle thrashed Port Vale 5-1 in a Second Division game at Vale Park. For more than half an hour, there was little to suggest the beating that was to come but the Pilgrims then netted four goals in 12 minutes. Marino Keith, David Friio and Steve Adams scored before the interval, with Paul Wotton adding the fourth in the first minute of the second half. Friio iced the cake with a long-range fifth.

WEDNESDAY 19TH OCTOBER 1904

Jack Picken scored his second hat-trick in a fortnight when Argyle beat Tottenham Hotspur 5-0 in a Western League game at Home Park. In keeping with clubs like Spurs, Argyle played in the Southern and Western Leagues, selecting the same players for both competitions.

TUESDAY 19TH OCTOBER 1982

The lowest crowd to witness a league game at Home Park – 2,525 – saw the Pilgrims beat AFC Bournemouth 2-0 in a Third Division game with goals from Kevin Hodges and John Sims. The early 1980s were the nadir for Argyle crowds – 15 of the lowest 18 Home Park attendances were recorded between 1981 and 1983.

SATURDAY 20TH OCTOBER 2007

Lee Martin netted on his full Argyle debut – and first match at Home Park – as the Pilgrims beat Coventry City 1-0 in the Championship. Martin, who made 12 appearances in a three-month loan spell from Manchester United, linked with former Old Trafford team-mate Sylvan Ebanks-Blake to score.

MONDAY 21ST OCTOBER 1940

Argyle beat Torquay United 4-0 in their first game in the South West Regional League, played after regular competition was suspended following the outbreak of World War II. Charles Sargeant scored twice.

SATURDAY 21ST OCTOBER 1995

Adrian Littlejohn claimed a hat-trick in a 4-0 victory over Devon neighbours Torquay United as the Pilgrims advanced to promotion from the Third Division under Neil Warnock. Littlejohn was top scorer as the Greens went up, scoring 17 times in his first season at Home Park.

SATURDAY 22ND OCTOBER 1994

At 16 years and 257 days, James Dungey became the youngest goalkeeper – and third-youngest player – to play for the Pilgrims when he came on as a sub in a 4-2 Second Division win at Stockport County. Plymouth-born Dungey, who made another 16 appearances, was called upon after regular custodian Alan Nichols was sent off for a second bookable offence.

WEDNESDAY 22ND OCTOBER 2003

Two headed goals from David Friio and a Paul Wotton penalty gave Argyle a 3-1 win at Sheffield Wednesday that took them to the top of the Second Division. The win culminated an extraordinary 11 days that saw the Pilgrims achieve four victories, score 18 goals, accumulate nine points, and progress in the LDV Vans Trophy at the expense of Bristol City.

SATURDAY 23RD OCTOBER 1926

Argyle lost 5-1 during one of their unproductive visits to Merthyr Town on their way to finishing Third Division (South) runners-up. It was Argyle's failure to beat Merthyr either home or away that cost the Pilgrims promotion.

TUESDAY 23RD OCTOBER 2007

Argyle won at the Valley for the first time in 33 years to beat Charlton Athletic 2-1. First-half goals from Sylvan Ebanks-Blake and Barry Hayles – either side of an unfortunate own goal by goalkeeper Luke McCormick when Danny Mills' strike hit the post and rebounded into the net off McCormick's head – assured Argyle of all three points. The Pilgrims' last away win against the Addicks had been at Selhurst Park during Charlton's exile from their home.

SATURDAY 24TH OCTOBER 1903

For the second successive Saturday, Argyle scored five goals to win a Southern League game. Seven days after beating Kettering 5-1 at Home Park, the Pilgrims went to Southampton and chalked up a 5-3 victory. Manager-to-be Robert Jack – Argyle's first professional – scored two goals against the Saints.

SATURDAY 24TH OCTOBER 1925

The goals went in two by two as the Pilgrims beat Bournemouth and Boscombe Athletic 7-2 in a Division Three (South) game at Home Park. Sammy Black, Jack Leslie, and Jack Cock all registered doubles, with Patsy Corcoran the only scorer not to pair up. It was the second time in a month that the Pilgrims had netted seven goals in a game, with Aberdare Athletic having been put to the sword five games previously.

SATURDAY 25TH OCTOBER 1947

Roy Nail made his one and only appearance for the Pilgrims in a 1-1 Second Division draw with Millwall at Home Park. Nail had been hammering in the goals for Cornish side St Blazey when he was plunged into the Pilgrims' first XI – following five games without an Argyle goal – but did not have the tools for league football and never played a professional game again.

SATURDAY 25TH OCTOBER 1969

Argyle beat Walsall 1-0 in a Third Division game at Home Park, thanks to Plymothian Steve Davey. Davey made his debut in 1967 after rising to the top by way of Plymouth Schoolboys and a Home Park apprenticeship. An England youth international, he switched from striker to full-back for two seasons, before resuming his forward role in time to spearhead the Pilgrims' run to the League Cup semi-final. After 55 goals in 249 appearances for Argyle, he played for Portsmouth and Hereford United.

SATURDAY 26TH OCTOBER 1929

Ray Bowden ensured he would never go short of a drink in Plymouth by scoring a hat-trick to help Argyle defeat their bitter Devonshire rivals Exeter City 4-1 in a Division Three (South) derby at Home Park. It was the second, and last, time an Argyle player scored three against the Grecians. Sammy Black was also on the scoresheet as the Pilgrims advanced on promotion to the Second Division after ten years of trying.

MONDAY 26TH OCTOBER 1953

Home Park's floodlights were turned on for the first time when the Pilgrims entertained Exeter City in a friendly. Only 2,025 people turned out to see Argyle shine 2-0, with goals from Maurice Tadman and Sam McCrory.

SATURDAY 27TH OCTOBER 1962

Wilf Carter scored the last of his eight hat-tricks as the Pilgrims recovered from conceding an early goal to defeat Charlton Athletic 6-1 in a Second Division game at Home Park. Carter liked playing against the Addicks, with this triple being his second against them and bringing his total in matches between the two sides to 13.

SATURDAY 27TH OCTOBER 1990

Goalkeeper Dave Walter made his debut for the Pilgrims in a 4-1 Second Division victory over Hull City at Home Park in which Danny Salman scored twice. Walter had been bought by David Kemp from Exeter City as a back-up for regular goalkeeper Rhys Wilmot and played 15 times in a year before moving to Torquay United.

SATURDAY 28TH OCTOBER 1939

Pat Glover scored a hat-trick as Argyle beat Bristol City 6-0 at Home Park in the second of the Pilgrims' games in the South West Regional League. Charles Sargeant, Jackie Smith and Harry Lane also scored.

SATURDAY 28TH OCTOBER 1950

Five second-half goals saw Argyle beat Football League new boys Colchester United 7-1 in a Third Division encounter at Home Park. There was little sign of the carnage to come at the interval, when Maurice Tadman had given the Pilgrims a 2-1 lead. Tadman and Billy Strauss each scored again after the break, with Neil Dougall, Alex Govan and George Dews also netting.

SATURDAY 29TH OCTOBER 1927

A Freddy Forbes hat-trick helped Argyle to a 4-2 Third Division (South) home win over Norwich City. Jack Leslie opened the scoring.

SATURDAY 29TH OCTOBER 1949

A Home Park crowd of 32,802 saw Argyle beat Preston North End 1-0 in a Second Division game. The reason for the interest was the visit of Preston's two England wingers, Bobby Langton and – especially – Tom Finney. The Pilgrims won with a Maurice Tadman goal.

TUESDAY 29TH OCTOBER 1996

Striker Lee Phillips became the youngest player to represent the Pilgrims in a senior game when he came on as a substitute, for Neil Illman, in a 2-0 Second Division victory over Gillingham at Home Park. At 16 years and 43 days, the Penzance-born schoolboy superseded Sam Shilton's previous lowest mark by nearly 100 days, and Michael Evans and Illman ensured a winning start to his 57-game Argyle career.

SATURDAY 30TH OCTOBER 1886

Argyle posted their first-ever win, in their third game, a 2-1 victory over Plymouth College. The line-up was: Gale, Lumm, Baker, Lew, Grose, Chapman, Dyer, Pethybridge, Boolds, Cornish, Vaughan. Grose and Chapman scored. Opponents for the remainder of the season included: Royal Artillery, Tavistock Grammar School, Mannamead School, Hotspur, Corporation Grammar School and Plymouth United.

TUESDAY 30TH OCTOBER 1973

Tony Waiter's Pilgrims continued their march to the semi-final of the League Cup when they won 2-1 at First Division Burnley. Having triumphed at Torquay United and beaten Portsmouth at Home Park, most thought Third Division Argyle's run would end at Turf Moor against a team in the top three of the top-flight and unbeaten at home for a year. After going behind, the Pilgrims levelled through Colin Waldron's own goal before Neil Hague grabbed a late winner.

SATURDAY 31ST OCTOBER 1903

Argyle's first FA Cup game as a professional side saw them beat Welsh side Whiteheads 7-0 in a first qualifying round tie at Home Park. Jack Peddie, Bob Dalrymple, and Herbert Winterhalder each scored twice as the Pilgrims began a run which went all the way to the first round proper, where they went out after a replay to The Wednesday – later to add a Sheffield prefix – that season's League champions.

WEDNESDAY 31ST OCTOBER 1906

H Swann scored all five goals as Argyle claimed a 5-0 home Western League victory over Millwall, who conceded just another ten goals in their other nine league games that season.

TUESDAY 31ST OCTOBER 2000

Paul Sturrock was appointed manager of Argyle following the dismissal of Kevin Hodges, with the club struggling to make an impact in the Third Division. After a transitional season, he steered the Pilgrims to the Third Division title, amassing 102 points. He guided Argyle to within touching distance of the Second Division championship two years later but left to take over Southampton 12 games before the end of the season. His defection did not diminish his standing with Argyle fans and he was voted manager of Argyle's Team of the Century. After further spells at Sheffield Wednesday and Swindon, 'Luggy' returned to Home Park for a second stint in charge.

PLYMOUTH ARGYLE
On This Day

P·A·F·C

NOVEMBER

WEDNESDAY 1st NOVEMBER 1961

Ellis Stuttard was promoted from assistant-trainer to Argyle manager, in succession to Neil Dougall, for the first of his two stints in the Home Park hot-seat. A former Argyle player, Stuttard came close to taking the Pilgrims into the top-flight with a fifth-place Second Division finish in his first season in charge, a position bettered only twice in the club's history.

SATURDAY 1st NOVEMBER 1975

Paul Mariner scored twice in the final 20 minutes as Argyle came from behind to earn a 2-2 Second Division draw against Chelsea at Stamford Bridge. Ian Britton gave the Blues an interval lead which Ray Wilkins added to against the run of play before the hour. Mariner converted Colin Randell's pass to score past veteran goalkeeper Peter Bonetti, and then headed home Hughie McAuley's cross.

SATURDAY 2nd NOVEMBER 1946

Bob Thomas scored two goals in Argyle's 4-1 defeat of Newport County in a Second Division match at Home Park. The 1946/47 season was the only one in which Bob played alongside his brother Dave in the Pilgrims' forward line, and the Londoners netted 36 goals between them. Older sibling Dave played 11 games the following season but Bob had already left the club by then, finding the lack of post-war accommodation in Plymouth a drawback and returning to the capital where he propelled Fulham to the Second Division title.

FRIDAY 2nd NOVEMBER 2001

Paul Sturrock picked up the Third Division Manager of the Month award for October – courtesy of the League's title sponsors Nationwide. A draw and four victories for the Pilgrims in October saw off the challenge of Luton Town's Joe Kinnear, Brian Talbot, of Rushden & Diamonds, and Exeter City's John Cornforth. "The constancy of the club is remarkable," said Chris Hull, of sponsors Nationwide. "Plymouth's record is phenomenal." In response, Sturrock was poetically doomy. "The thing about tidal waves is that they end up crashing on the rocks," he said.

SATURDAY 3RD NOVEMBER 1984

Goalkeeper Les Sealey made the last of his six appearances for the Pilgrims in a 3-2 home Third Division victory over Bristol Rovers. Sealey, who was on loan from Luton Town, was following in the studmarks of cousin Alan, who had joined Argyle from West Ham United seven years earlier. Alan, a forward who won a European Cup-Winners' Cup winners' medal with the Hammers, made just four appearances for Argyle before injury forced his retirement. Sealey sadly died aged just 43, while still employed as a coach at Upton Park.

TUESDAY 3RD NOVEMBER 1998

The shooting star that was Darren Bastow made a scoring debut as a 16-year-old in the Pilgrims' 3-0 Third Division victory over Brentford. At 16 years and 316 days, he is the youngest-ever scorer in Argyle history. The Torquinian midfielder seemed to have the world at his talented feet, with Premiership teams falling over themselves to invite 'the new Paul Gascoigne' for trials. Yet, little more than a year, 52 games, and three more goals, later, the still teenaged Bastow walked out on the professional game forever, despite a brief attempt to resurrect his career when former youth-team mentor Kevin Summerfield returned to Home Park with Paul Sturrock. "I just did not want to play football anymore," was his explanation. "I just got fed up with it all."

SATURDAY 4TH NOVEMBER 1933

Argyle scored four goals away from home in a Second Division fixture at Hull City, but still came away with nothing, losing 5-4 on Humberside. Jimmy Cookson netted twice, with Frank Sloan and Sammy Black also on the mark.

WEDNESDAY 4TH NOVEMBER 1964

Argyle's progress to the semi-final of the League Cup was briefly halted by top-flight Stoke City, who scored a controversial late fourth round equaliser to secure a 1-1 draw at the Victoria Ground. With three minutes to go, Malcolm Allison's Second Division Pilgrims led the previous season's finalists through a Frank Lord goal but were pegged back by John Ritchie, who fouled goalkeeper Dave MacLaren and defender Cliff Jackson in scoring.

SATURDAY 5TH NOVEMBER 1960

Ken 'Bugsy' Maloy made his debut in a 4-0 Second Division defeat by Liverpool. Maloy, a Londoner, joined Argyle as a teenager from Ilford and made 74 appearances for the Pilgrims across four seasons before leaving. He later played abroad in Belgium for the best part of a decade.

SATURDAY 5TH NOVEMBER 1988

Tommy Tynan became only the third Pilgrim since the Second World War to score four goals in a game as Second Division Argyle beat Blackburn Rovers 4-3 at Home Park. Remarkably, he was just a fortnight short of his 33rd birthday. Even more remarkably, the ball with which he scored all four goals was booted out of Home Park during the match but was returned to him after an appeal in the local Western Morning News.

THURSDAY 6TH NOVEMBER 2003

French midfielder David Friio was named the Umbro Isotonic Second Division Player of the Month for October. Friio was praised by judges of the award for being: "simply outstanding during Argyle's rise to the top of the table." He scored five goals during the month, including doubles in away wins at Port Vale and Sheffield Wednesday.

SATURDAY 6TH NOVEMBER 2004

Argyle ended Wigan Athletic's season-long unbeaten Championship run on their first visit to the JJB Stadium, winning 2-0. Goals from Paul Wotton and substitute Stevie Crawford ensured victory over a Latics' side that had gone 18 games since previously tasting defeat and that ended the season as runners-up. The Wigan line-up included future Pilgrim Gary Teale.

SATURDAY 7TH NOVEMBER 1914

Bert Bowler scored four goals as Argyle beat Southampton 6-2 in a Southern League match at Home Park. Bowler, who was discovered by manager Bob Jack playing for Army Cup winners Sherwood Foresters, represented England in an unofficial international against Scotland in Cairo during World War I. Harry Raymond and Tommy Gallogley scored the other two goals.

SATURDAY 7TH NOVEMBER 1931

Argyle were held to a 1-1 Second Division draw by Burnley after a thrice-taken penalty. Leading at Turf Moor by Sammy Black's goal, the Pilgrims conceded a spot-kick before the hour when Harry Bland handled. George Waterfield took the penalty which was turned aside by goalkeeper Harry Cann. Cann moved early, so the kick was retaken. Same players, same result. With Waterfield's confidence shot, Peter O'Dowd assumed responsibility and scored.

TUESDAY 7TH NOVEMBER 1995

Neil Warnock made Keith Hill his captain in an Auto Windscreens Shield game against Northampton Town at Sixfields… and then promptly substituted him 26 minutes into the 1-0 defeat. "Obviously his mind was not on the game, so it was pointless him carrying on," said Warnock. Argyle went out of the competition 1-0 after Richard Logan had been sent off.

FRIDAY 8TH NOVEMBER 1991

David Regis made his Argyle debut as the Pilgrims lost a Second Division clash at Tranmere Rovers, 1-0. Regis, who had scored a hat-trick for Notts County against the Pilgrims the previous season, was a David Kemp signing after Dan McCauley took over as chairman, and the expectation that came with being the club's first major purchase for several seasons weighed heavily on the shoulders of the big striker, who scored four goals in 31 games.

SATURDAY 8TH NOVEMBER 1997

Lee Hodges became the second player with that name to represent the club, when made his Argyle debut in a 3-0 Second Division home win against AFC Bournemouth. Argyle have had two players called Lee Hodges – both born in London – and they played for the club in three spells, spanning 15 years around the turn of the Millennium. One had a seven-game spell on loan from Tottenham Hotspur in 1993, before the second had a nine-game stint, also on loan, from West Ham United in 1997. Then the first one rejoined the Pilgrims and went on to be an integral part of the 2001/02 and 2003/04 promotion teams, playing 215 games. The second Lee Hodges made a career for himself at Scunthorpe United.

SATURDAY 9TH NOVEMBER 1957

A contentious second goal condemned Argyle to a Third Division (South) defeat at Brentford. Already 1-0 down and chasing the game, the Pilgrims went further behind when goalkeeper Harry Brown was rendered unconscious as he challenged for the ball. As the knocked-out custodian dropped to the ground, Brentford striker George Francis knocked the ball home and the referee cold-heartedly allowed it to give the Bees a 2-0 victory.

SATURDAY 9TH NOVEMBER 1968

Ivan Robinson 'scored' the most infamous goal in Argyle's history to give Barrow a 1-0 Third Division victory at Holker Street. Robinson played neither for Barrow nor for Argyle but was the match referee and, of course, he did not score. He did, though, deflect George McLean's shot past wrong-footed Pilgrims' custodian Pat Dunne. The shot had been going well wide when, according to the man in black, it "hit the inside of my left foot and flew off at a peculiar angle".

SATURDAY 10TH NOVEMBER 1923

A much-vaunted forward – a non-league find from Chorley – Albert Fishwick preceded Paul Mariner by half a century when he made his Argyle debut in a 1-0 Third Division (South) defeat at Northampton Town. Sadly for Albert and romantics everywhere, he failed to blaze that trail any further and, after just seven games and one goal, returned to the north-west to find the goals for Blackpool. He proved he might have been the Fishwick that got away, though, scoring 36 times in 49 league appearances.

TUESDAY 10TH NOVEMBER 1987

In their first appearance in the short-lived cup tournament the Simod Cup – which included First and Second Division teams – Argyle were beaten 6-2 by Manchester City at Maine Road. It was the second of three times that Argyle lost on Moss Side that season, being sandwiched between a 2-1 Second Division defeat on the opening day and a later FA Cup fifth round reversal, by 3-1. Argyle's only other Simod Cup outing came a year later, when they also lost 6-2, at Chelsea.

SATURDAY 10TH NOVEMBER 2007

The Pilgrims' 3-0 Championship victory over Norwich City at Home Park produced two separate talking points – one good, one bad. The second goal, by Paul Connolly, was the full-back's first and only strike in nearly 180 first-team games for the Pilgrims; while the match was Ian Holloway's last as manager before he surprisingly walked out on the club for a short and ill-starred reign in charge of Leicester City.

SATURDAY 11TH NOVEMBER 1899

Wing-half Jimmy Dickinson, who helped Argyle bridge the divide between the Southern League and the Football League, was born. The Royal Navy discovery became a key Pilgrim immediately after the First World War and was a member of the first Argyle league team in 1920. He had five seasons of Third Division (South) football, making 111 appearances, before leaving for Wigan Borough.

WEDNESDAY 11TH NOVEMBER 1964

Malcolm Allison's Second Division Argyle claimed a second First Division League Cup scalp as Frank Lord's hat-trick – the first by an Argyle player in the competition – knocked First Division Stoke City out of the competition 3-1 in a fourth round replay at Home Park. Lord claimed his fifth, sixth and seventh goals in that season's League Cup before Stoke's Peter Dobing finally found a way past Pilgrims' goalkeeper Dave MacLaren, who played with a broken nose that he picked up during the previous week's draw in the Potteries.

SATURDAY 12TH NOVEMBER 1955

Argyle twice came from behind to beat Leeds United 4-3 in a pulsating Second Division clash at Home Park. The struggling Pilgrims went behind when defender George Robertson put through his own net but led at half-time thanks to goals from George Willis and Johnny Williams. Leeds levelled after the interval and then took the lead through John Charles before Eric Davis put Argyle back on terms, setting the stage for Neil Dougall to hit the winner. The victory was one of the few bright spots in a season which eventually saw Argyle relegated.

SATURDAY 12TH NOVEMBER 1960

Argyle saved everything for the second half of their Division Two derby against Bristol Rovers at Eastville. After going in to the break 1-0 down, they produced a blistering display in the second 45 minutes to win 5-2. Pirates defender Ted Purdon set them on their way with an oggie, and Wilf Carter, George Kirby, Johnny Williams and Jimmy McAnearney took their cue from him.

SATURDAY 13TH NOVEMBER 1971

Argyle were so impressed by the scorer of the winning goal in a 4-3 Division Three defeat by Rotherham United that they bought the player. In truth, substitute Neil Hague, the executioner of the injury-time winner at Millmoor, had been in discussions about a move to Home Park before the game, so there was no real surprise when he agreed terms after downing his future employers. Hughie Reed, Bobby Saxton and Derek Rickard had given Argyle a 3-2 lead – after being 2-0 down – with nine minutes to go before Bobby Ham equalised.

SATURDAY 13TH NOVEMBER 1976

A huge crowd of over 25,000 packed into Home Park for a mid-table Second Division game against Fulham that ended 2-2. The attraction was to be found among the names in the in opposition line-up: former England captain and World Cup winner Bobby Moore, legendary wing-wizard George Best and entertaining playmaker Rodney Marsh. Argyle's Terry Austin and Brian Johnson ensured the share of the spoils, if not the crowd's admiration.

SUNDAY 14TH NOVEMBER 1999

Striker Paul McGregor scored Argyle's final hat-trick of the 20th century when the Pilgrims beat Barnet 4-1 in a Third Division game. Ian Stonebridge completed the scoring. Most people knew two things about McGregor, who was the Greens' top scorer in the 1999-2000 season, with 16 goals. Firstly, that he scored Nottingham Forest's winning goal against Olympique Lyonnais in the 1995-96 Uefa Cup to put Forest in the quarter-finals of the competition. And secondly, that he sang with Britpop band Merc, although the group did not have any commercial success.

SATURDAY 15TH NOVEMBER 1952

A controversial late goal from Neil Dougall gave Argyle a 1-0 victory over Everton in a Second Division game at Home Park. Pilgrims' goalkeeper Bill Shortt saved a penalty from Tommy Clinton before Dougall scored after the referee had blown his whistle for a foul. Everton's players stopped, expecting a free-kick as Dougall smashed the ball past goalkeeper Ted Sagar.

SATURDAY 15TH NOVEMBER 1986

A stunning shot from 35-year-old defender Gordon Nisbet gave Argyle a 1-0 home Second Division victory against the veteran Nisbet's former employers West Bromwich Albion. 'Nizzie' had already racked up a century of appearances for Albion (including making his debut for the club as a goalkeeper) and nearly doubled that at Hull City before coming to Home Park. Already 29 when he signed for Argyle, he just kept going and going. By the time they wrenched his boots off him in 1987 he had played 322 times and scored 14 goals. He went on to look after the youth team, was briefly caretaker-manager, and was a shoo-in for the Team of the Century's right-back.

SATURDAY 16TH NOVEMBER 1912

Bert Bowler scored a hat-trick as Argyle won 4-0 against Stoke City on their way to the Southern League title. Bowler, who played for the Pilgrims as an amateur while serving in the Army, was a regular member of the Southern League representative side that played against the Football League

WEDNESDAY 16TH NOVEMBER 1960

Argyle chairman Ron Blindell slated the Pilgrims' stayaway fans after the Greens dumped Birmingham City out of the first League Cup. The Second Division Pilgrims' produced a cup giant-killing in beating the Blues 3-1 in a third round replay at Home Park – and that despite giving the First Division side a start through Reg Wyatt's own goal. Wilf Carter, George Kirby and Cliff Jackson turned things round in front of a crowd of little more than 14,000, leaving chairman Blindell to bemoan: "Where are the fans? I just can't understand why they stayed at home."

THURSDAY 17TH NOVEMBER 1955

Thomas Edward Tynan, Argyle's greatest striker of the modern era, was born in Liverpool. Tynan enjoyed two spells at Home Park – 1983-1985 and 1986-1990 – and his career can be summed up in stats – 262 league appearances; 126 league goals; 31 goals in the 1984/85 season; 24 in the 1988/89 season; Argyle Player of the Season 1984/85, 1986/87, and 1988/89; and leading Argyle goalscorer in 1983/84, 1984/85, 1986/87, 1987/88, 1988/89, and 1989/90. He was a member of the side which reached the 1984 FA Cup semi-final, scoring the goal that beat West Bromwich Albion in the fifth round, and helped Dave Smith's side win promotion to the Second Division in 1986 with 10 goals in nine games on loan from Rotherham United.

SATURDAY 17TH NOVEMBER 1990

Paul Robinson marked his full debut by scoring twice as Argyle overcame Millwall 3-2 in a Second Division encounter at Home Park. The tall 19-year-old announced his arrival in an Argyle starting line-up in a manner that he could not come close to repeating, and went on to make just six further starts in his Pilgrims' career before leaving for Hereford United the following summer. Nicky Marker scored the Greens' other goal, while Teddy Sheringham was on target for Millwall.

SATURDAY 18TH NOVEMBER 1950

For the second time in six games, Maurice Tadman scored four times for the Pilgrims. A month after putting four past Aldershot at Home Park, Tadman mined his golden seam at the Goldstone Ground, where Argyle won a Third Division (South) game against Brighton & Hove Albion 6-0. Billy Strauss and Sid Rundle were the supporting scorers as Tadman took his tally to 14 goals in seven matches.

WEDNESDAY 18TH NOVEMBER 1953

Argyle played host to Austrian side Admira Vienna in a friendly at Home Park. The Austrians who, according to a local newspaper correspondent of the time, "were not good tacklers and they didn't like to be tackled", won 4-2.

WEDNESDAY 19TH NOVEMBER 1958

A memorable day for forward Barrie Meyer, as he scored an impressive FA Cup hat-trick as Argyle beat Gillingham 4-1 in a first round replay at Priestfield following a 2-2 draw. Meyer had joined Argyle from Bristol Rovers, for whom he had played for ten years while also representing Gloucestershire at county cricket – but he found it difficult to adapt to life in the real Westcountry. He ended with an excellent goals-to-games ratio, however, having scored eight goals in just ten games during his six-month stay with the Pilgrims.

SATURDAY 19TH NOVEMBER 1983

The greatest FA Cup run in Argyle's history began in fairly inauspicious circumstances with a 0-0 draw at Southend United. Villa Park seemed a long way away as two teams at the wrong end of the Third Division slugged it out for 90 minutes without managing a goal between them. However, ten of the men who started at Roots Hall were in Argyle's 12-man squad for the following spring's semi-final. Tony Kellow was the exception.

TUESDAY 20TH NOVEMBER 1973

Underdogs Argyle reached the quarter-final stage of the League Cup by knocking out top-flight Queens Park Rangers with three second-half goals at Loftus Road. Tony Waiters' Third Division side knocked out a Rangers' team – containing such luminaries as Stan Bowles, Terry Venables, Frank McLintock, Phil Parkes and Don Givens – and progressed thanks to a double from Alan Welsh either side of Steve Davey's strike.

SATURDAY 20TH NOVEMBER 1993

Striker Dwight Marshall scored a hat-trick as Argyle won 5-1 at Bradford City in a season when they agonisingly missed out on automatic promotion to the Second Division by a single victory and then failed in the play-offs. This despite being the division's leading scorers with a huge tally of 88 goals. Marshall, who had two spells at Home Park, scored his fair share of them, as did his partner Kevin Nugent, who also netted against the Bantams after defender Andy Comyn had opened the scoring.

SATURDAY 21st NOVEMBER 1964

Mike Trebilcock scored twice as Argyle beat Manchester City 3-2 in a Second Division clash at Home Park. The one that had the country talking came after Argyle won a penalty, which saw Johnny Newman tap the ball forward a couple of yards from the spot. Enter the on-rushing Trebilcock to fire past goalkeeper Alan Ogley for a perfectly executed goal. The goal was a reprise of one that Newman had previously been involved in with team-mate Wilf Carter.

WEDNESDAY 21st NOVEMBER 2007

Ian Holloway resigned as Argyle manager to take charge of Leicester City. Rumours that Holloway had been contemplating leaving Home Park had previously been dismissed by the man himself, unequivocally. "Anyone who takes that seriously ought to commit themselves to an asylum," he said.

SATURDAY 22nd NOVEMBER 1947

Argyle ended a run of nine Second Division matches without victory when they defeated Southampton 3-1 at Home Park. It was the Pilgrims' third win of the campaign and the first time that they had scored more than a single goal in a match. Frank Squires, Maurice Tadman and Billy Strauss laid the bogey.

TUESDAY 22nd NOVEMBER 1983

Argyle were given a helping hand on their road to the FA cup semi-final as they beat fellow Third Division side Southend United 2-0 in a first round replay at Home Park. Shrimpers' defender Micky Stead set them on their way with an own goal, with Tommy Tynan adding the second.

TUESDAY 23rd NOVEMBER 1937

Jim Furnell, the most popular goalkeeper in Argyle's history, was born in Manchester. Furnell was nearly 33 when he made his Pilgrims' debut in 1970 after joining for a snip from Arsenal, but still managed to rack up 206 appearances before he retired with his 39th birthday looming. The Green Army loved him, making him Player of the Year in his first full season, and voting him into the number one position in the Argyle Team of the Century.

SATURDAY 23rd NOVEMBER 1974

The Dream Duo of Paul Mariner and Billy Rafferty each scored a late goal as Argyle staved off embarrassment in an FA Cup first round tie at Dartford. The Southern League side led the Pilgrims – who were on their way to promotion to the Second Division – 2-1 after Tommy Henderson scored in the 86th minute. Time enough, still, for Mariner to head home substitute Alan Rogers' delivery, and Rafferty to then deflect Colin Randell's cross to give Argyle a 3-2 win and deny Dartford the cachet of being the first non-league side to knock the Pilgrims out of the Cup.

SATURDAY 24th NOVEMBER 1934

Eugene Melaniphy scored one of Argyle's two goals in their 3-2 Second Division defeat by Bolton Wanderers, the third away match in a row that the County Mayo-born forward had scored. 'Miffy' as his mouthful of a surname was abbreviated to, scored eight goals in seven consecutive games that autumn/winter; the second-best scoring streak in the Pilgrims' history.

SATURDAY 24th NOVEMBER 1973

Future Argyle assistant-manager Stewart Houston fired the Pilgrims into the second round of the FA Cup with a super strike… into his own goal. Argyle beat Brentford 2-1 after Houston, taking a sojourn at Griffin Park between spells at Chelsea and Manchester United, smashed home the winner from 30 yards three minutes from time.

SATURDAY 25th NOVEMBER 1950

Argyle won an FA Cup tie for the first time in nearly 14 years when yet another Maurice Tadman hat-trick gave them a comfortable 3-0 first-round win at Gainsborough Trinity.

WEDNESDAY 25th NOVEMBER 1964

Argyle reached the semi-final of the League Cup for the first time when they knocked fellow Second Division side Northampton Town out 1-0 in front of a near 22,000 crowd at Home Park. The Cobblers came to the Westcountry unbeaten in 18 games but had no answer to Johnny Newman's early goal.

SATURDAY 25TH NOVEMBER 1978

For the first time in their history, Argyle were knocked out of the FA Cup by a non-league side. Malcolm Allison's Third Division outfit were humiliated 2-0 at Southern League Worcester City in a first-round tie.

TUESDAY 26TH NOVEMBER 1935

Defender Doug Baird was born in Falkirk. Baird, a Scottish under-23 international, was taken to Home Park by Andy Beattie, for whom he had previously played at Nottingham Forest. The ex-Partick Thistle full-back played 158 times for the Greens between 1963 and 1968.

SATURDAY 26TH NOVEMBER 1983

Argyle's Third Division game against Wimbledon was abandoned after 27 minutes when referee Keith Cooper called a halt to proceedings at a sopping wet Home Park. The decision was disputed by Dons' manager Dave Bassett, as well as angry fans, all of who pointed out that the conditions had not deteriorated following the kick-off. The fans were mollified when Argyle chairman Stuart Dawe agreed to admit them for half-price when the game was replayed in April, while Bassett was presumably happy with the 2-1 win then.

SATURDAY 27TH NOVEMBER 1909

Harry Raymond scored twice as Argyle beat Coventry City 6-0 in a Southern League game at Home Park. It was former Mutley Grammar School captain Raymond's first full season for the Greens and he stayed with the club for 16 years, winning three England amateur caps and turning professional when the club entered the Football League before leaving to become Torquay United's player-manager. For his sterling service, he was granted a benefit match against crack amateur side Corinthians.

TUESDAY 27TH NOVEMBER 2007

Paul Sturrock was appointed Argyle manager for the second time, moving back to Home Park from Swindon Town. He brought with him coaches Kevin Summerfield and John Blackley, who were his right and left-hand men during his first spell in Devon, and the trio steered the Greens through choppy waters to tenth place in the Championship, their highest league finish for 21 years.

SATURDAY 28TH NOVEMBER 1925

Argyle and Crystal Palace shared ten goals on snow-covered Selhurst Park as their Third Division (South) encounter ended 5-5. In the ultimate game of two halves, Argyle led 4-1 at the interval, thanks to Patsy Corcoran, Freddy Forbes and Jack Cock (2). Palace's strike came from ex-Argyle forward Percy Cherrett. Remarkably, though, with the 90 minutes up, the Pilgrims trailed 5-4. Enter Sammy Black to bring the Greens level with the final kick of the game.

SATURDAY 28TH NOVEMBER 1936

Argyle came from behind to beat Tottenham Hotspur 3-1 in a Second Division game in front of 33,000 at White Hart Lane. The Pilgrims recovered from George Hunt's early strike to equalise through Jackie Smith and then take the lead when Johnny McNeil netted a clever free-kick. John Connor headed a third after the break.

THURSDAY 29TH NOVEMBER 1979

Adam Barrett, whose Argyle career spanned two centuries, was born in Dagenham. Barrett made his debut as a substitute on trial from Leyton Orient in a 5-0 Third Division victory over Scunthorpe United at Home Park in March 1999. The following season, he returned to Devon on a permanent basis and played 38 times under Kevin Hodges. It was the arrival of Paul Sturrock, and another five-for – this time by Cheltenham Town in a 5-2 defeat of the Pilgrims at Whaddon Road – that put paid to Barrett's time at Argyle and he left for Mansfield Town.

SATURDAY 30TH NOVEMBER 1912

Argyle lost a Southern League game against Reading 1-0 at Home Park to surrender a 25-match unbeaten home run that extended back 14 months to the opening day of the previous campaign.

SATURDAY 30TH NOVEMBER 1974

Striker Barrie Vassallo made his debut in a 2-2 home Third Division draw with Chesterfield, as substitute for Billy Rafferty. Vassallo began his career as an apprentice at Arsenal but failed to break into the first team at Highbury, moving to Argyle in November 1974. His appearances at Argyle were limited and he moved on to Torquay United after two years.

PLYMOUTH ARGYLE
On This Day

DECEMBER

SATURDAY 1st DECEMBER 1962

Alan O'Neill marked his Argyle debut with a late equaliser in a 1-1 draw at Chelsea. The £8,000 purchase from Aston Villa levelled Frank Blunstone's opener with three minutes to play in the Second Division game and went on to be an ever-present for the next year, scoring 14 goals, before leaving for AFC Bournemouth.

SATURDAY 1st DECEMBER 1984

The Pilgrims won 2-0 in a Third Division game at Swansea City, their first away league win for 13 months, with goals from Gordon Staniforth and Tommy Tynan. The game was the second of Dave Smith's managerial reign. Smith, who played for Burnley, Brighton & Hove Albion, and Bristol City during his career as a full-back, managed Mansfield Town out of the Fourth Division and led Southend United to two promotions before joining Argyle following 16 months out of the game. He took the Pilgrims to the Second Division in 1986 before an offer from his hometown club Dundee saw him leave Home Park in 1988.

SATURDAY 2nd DECEMBER 1989

Irish international defender Jim Beglin made his Argyle debut in a 3-2 Second Division defeat at Oxford. Beglin, Bob Paisley's last signing for Liverpool, had been brought to Home Park from Leeds United by manager Ken Brown to bring some of his experience to help steady a struggling Argyle a side that had won just once in their previous seven games. However, the left-back had never really recovered from a broken leg sustained in a clash with Everton's Gary Stevens during a Merseyside derby two years previously and he did little to help the Pilgrims. They lost three and drew two of the games in which Beglin played. The former Red retired soon afterwards to pursue a successful career in television punditry.

SATURDAY 2nd DECEMBER 2000

Two Sean McCarthy goals saw the first Paul Sturrock-selected league side get the new boss off to a winning start with a 2-0 victory over arch rivals Exeter City at St James's Park in the Third Division. Defenders David Worrell and Brian McGlinchey, and midfielder David Friio made Pilgrims' debuts.

SATURDAY 3rd DECEMBER 1910

Argyle lost 6-1 away to Coventry City in a Southern League match at Highfield Road, Fred Burch's goal proving their only consolation. The Greens got their revenge later in the season when they also hit the Sky Blues for six. Nine Pilgrims featured in both matches.

WEDNESDAY 3rd DECEMBER 1924

Crawford Clelland, the only player born in the USA to represent Argyle, was born in New Jersey. Clelland's parents were Scottish and he joined Argyle from Aberdeen in 1955, but played in just two Second Division games at the beginning of the season – both defeats, at Sheffield Wednesday and home to Nottingham Forest, respectively – before being sent back over the border.

SATURDAY 3rd DECEMBER 1994

Sam Shilton, son of manager Peter, became the youngest player to represent the Pilgrims in an FA Cup tie when he came on as a substitute in a 2-1 second-round victory over AFC Bournemouth at Home Park, aged 16 years and 145 days.

TUESDAY 4th DECEMBER 1923

Lou Tinkler, by common consent one of the few bright spots in the gloomy post Second World War season of 1946-47, was born in Chester-le-Street. Despite his music-hall name, Tinkler was spotted by Argyle manager Jack Tresadern after being posted to Plymouth by the Royal Navy in 1942. A diminutive winger, Tinkler never really displaced Strauss in Tresadern's affections after scoring four goals in 24 games in the season that league football resumed, and moved on to Walsall.

TUESDAY 4th DECEMBER 2007

Argyle announced the appointment of former Everton midfielder and Swindon Town manager Andy King as their chief scout. Apart from scoring a spectacular goal to win the 1978 Merseyside derby at Goodison, King's main claim to fame is being the first player to score a Football League goal on an artificial surface when he netted against Luton Town at Loftus Road on September 1, 1981, although Rangers lost 2-1 in front of a 19,000 crowd.

SATURDAY 5TH DECEMBER 1903

Wattie Anderson scored the first-ever hat-trick by an Argyle professional player. He scored his triple in a 4-1 Southern League victory over Wellingborough at Home Park.

SATURDAY 5TH DECEMBER 1931

Ray Bowden was on target with a treble as Argyle blew away Southampton 6-0 in a Second Division game at The Dell. In addition to Bowden's hat-trick Jack Vidler scored twice, with Sammy Black also on target. It was young Cornishman Bowden's last full season for the Pilgrims before he was snapped up by Arsenal for a club-record fee for the Gunners of £5,000. A year later, he won the first of six England caps and went on to play for Newcastle United before returning to the Westcountry – not a bad career for someone nursed along by Argyle because they felt he might be a little too slight for the game.

SATURDAY 6TH DECEMBER 1930

Argyle overcame the odds to inflict a 2-0 defeat on Tottenham Hotspur at Home Park. Going into the match it was a daunting task facing a Pilgrims' side without a win in eight Second Division games – and was made seemingly impossible when they lost goalkeeper Harry Cann through injury after half an hour of the match. With no replacements in 1930, Freddie Titmuss went in goal and forward Jack Leslie moved to centre-half, Argyle refused to sit back and were rewarded with goals from Tommy Grozier and Sammy Black – his 100th league goal.

MONDAY 6TH DECEMBER 2004

Argyle announced the appointment of a new chief executive, Michael Dunford, who had previously held a similar post at Everton for ten years before leaving Goodison Park the previous summer. Dunford, who started his long and distinguished career in football administration at Derby County, took up his new position the following month. He had been sat in the Home Park directors' box the previous on Saturday – alongside the Wales manager John Toshack – to watch the Pilgrims beat Burnley 1-0 in a Championship clash.

SATURDAY 7TH DECEMBER 1957

It was certainly a day for Argyle goals in the FA Cup, as they knocked non-league Dorchester Town out of the competition with a 5-2 second-round victory at Home Park, in which Wilf Carter scored the first of two hat-tricks in successive weeks. Harry Penk and Jimmy Gauld were the supporting cast. With two goals against Watford in a 6-2 first-round win, and the Pilgrims' lone strike in a third round 6-1 thrashing by Newcastle United, Carter claimed six goals in a tournament which saw the Pilgrims' three games realise a total of 22 goals.

SATURDAY 7TH DECEMBER 1963

A 1-0 home defeat by Leeds equalled the club record of nine consecutive league defeats. The Pilgrims had last won a Second Division game on October 5, after which, following a draw at Manchester City, they lost at home to Northampton Town, Swindon Town, Portsmouth, Norwich City and were defeated at Sunderland, Rotherham United, Scunthorpe United and Cardiff City.

SATURDAY 8TH DECEMBER 1923

Percy Cherrett scored twice as Argyle beat Queens Park Rangers 2-0 in a Third Division (South) game at Home Park. The following week, Cherrett also scored twice, in a 2-1 win away at Newport County. The following week, Cherrett also scored twice, in a 3-2 home win over Newport. Three days later, Cherrett also scored twice, in a 4-0 home win over Exeter City. The following day, Cherrett also scored twice, in a 4-0 away win over Exeter City. Three days later, Cherrett did not score and Argyle did not win.

SATURDAY 8TH DECEMBER 1990

Scottish international Brian McAllister made his debut for the Pilgrims in a 2-0 Second Division defeat at parent club Wimbledon. Borrowed by David Kemp from the Dons, McAllister made eight appearances during his loan spell at Home Park. He went on to bigger and better things after returning to Wimbledon, where he featured regularly in the Premiership, and won three Scottish caps, all in 1997: against Belarus, Malta and Wales, before being forced to retire in 2000 with a heel injury.

SATURDAY 9TH DECEMBER 1961

A huge crowd of almost 13,000 packed Home Park for a reserve-team game against Tottenham Hotspur, while the first team played away at Anfield. The game was the first in England for Jimmy Greaves, following his £99,999 return from Italy. The 'Man from Milan' seemed embarrassed by his reception, which included a toe-curling introduction from Argyle chairman Ron Blindell – "On behalf of Devon and Cornwall, the west of England... nay, the whole of England..." – but it did not stop him scoring twice in a 4-1 Football Combination win.

TUESDAY 9TH DECEMBER 1975

Argyle lost 2-1 to Manchester United in a benefit game for Peter Middleton. Middleton scored on his Pilgrims' debut, a 3-0 Third Division win over Shrewsbury Town – after moving to Home Park from Bradford City – but never played again. A few days later, he was knocked down by a car, badly damaged his back and, after futile attempts to resurrect his career, quit on the advice of a specialist. In 1977, after suffering from depression brought on by the sudden end to his career, Middleton took his own life.

SUNDAY 10TH DECEMBER 1939

David Burnside, a most skilful Pilgrim, was born in Kingswood, Gloucestershire. Burnside came to the Home Park crowd's notice before he played for the first team, when he entertained them with his ball-juggling skills at half-time. Such were his skills that he won a national newspaper contest to find the top pro at keepie-uppie; his 495 consecutive headers trounced runner-up Tommy Hamer, of Tottenham Hotspur, by more than 200. There was more to Burnside than party tricks, however. He made 113 appearances over four Home Park seasons, scoring 17 goals, and was Player of the Year in 1969.

SATURDAY 10TH DECEMBER 1983

Argyle saw off non-league Barking 2-1 in the second round of their run to the FA Cup semi-final. Fewer than 5,000 came to Home Park to see the Pilgrims come out on top against the Barking underdogs with goals from Mark Rowe and Lindsay Smith.

SATURDAY 11TH DECEMBER 1886

Argyle played Plymouth United in the first derby between the two sides at "the Argyle Ground – Mount Gould". United were formed before Argyle – who did not use the 'Plymouth' prefix until several years later – and were a pioneering club: they are believed to be one of the first, if not the first, team to use the now ubiquitous 'United' suffix. On this occasion Argyle won 4-1, with two goals each for Babb and Pethybridge.

SATURDAY 11TH DECEMBER 1920

David Jack, or, to give him his full name, David Bone Nightingale Jack, made the last of his 14 Football League appearances for the Greens in a 0-0 Third Division draw with Southend United at Home Park. The manager's son was then sold to Bolton Wanderers, for £3,000, and went on to make football history: he scored Bolton's two goals in their 2-0 win against West Ham in Wembley's first, 'White Horse', FA Cup Final in 1923. After another FA Cup Final with Wanderers, Jack joined Arsenal for a record £10,890, won three league titles, two more FA Cups and a total of nine England caps. Ironically, he lost his place in the Gunners' side to another ex-Argyle player, Ray Bowden.

FRIDAY 12TH DECEMBER 1952

Colin Randell, who played 277 times for the Pilgrims in two separate spells with the club in the 1970s and 1980s, was born in Neath, Wales. Randell made his Pilgrims' debut in October 1973 and was a pivotal player in Argyle's run to the semi-final of the League Cup that season, and played a big part in the following year's promotion to the Second Division. He left Home Park in 1977 to sign for Devonshire rivals Exeter City but eventually saw the error of his ways after a couple of seasons at St James's Park and returned in July 1979. Argyle paid heavily for letting Welsh under-23 international Randell move up the A38, selling him to the Grecians for £10,000 and buying him back for £60,000. He played for the club for another three years having been brought back by his former Argyle team-mate and Exeter boss Bobby Saxton. Saxton left Argyle for Blackburn Rovers in 1981 and signed Randell again when he took him to Ewood Park a year later.

SATURDAY 12TH DECEMBER 1959

If you wanted to see goals around Christmas time of the 1959-60 season, it was worth following Argyle. A 6-1 defeat at Swansea Town – Wilf Carter scoring – came in the middle of a sequence of ten Pilgrims' games in which 51 goals were scored; 20 by Argyle and 31 by their opponents.

TUESDAY 13TH DECEMBER 1960

Ace goalscorer Wilf Carter showed another side to his talents when he took over in goal for 20 minutes as Argyle shocked First Division Aston Villa by holding them to a 3-3 League Cup draw. Carter went between the posts in the fourth round tie at Villa Park when goalkeeper Geoff Barnsley had his nose broken by Gerry Hitchens. It was a fine achievement to get a draw against Villa, as the Pilgrims also carried the injured Bill Wright as a virtual passenger for the entire second half. Argyle led 3-2 thanks to goals from Carter, Peter Anderson and Johnny Williams, but the game was taken back to Home Park by Jimmy McEwan's second-half equaliser.

SATURDAY 13TH DECEMBER 2003

In a dramatic Second Division clash at Swindon Town, Argyle threw away a 2-0 lead before hitting back to win the game 3-2 in injury-time. Tony Capaldi and David Norris put the Pilgrims 2-0 up at the County Ground before the home side rallied and levelled; future Home Park hero Rory Fallon getting on the scoresheet. Swindon were still complaining about the sending-off of Steve Robinson when Marino Keith strode forward to smash in the winner: 2-2 and they mucked it up!

SATURDAY 14TH DECEMBER 1957

Hat-trick specialist Wilf Carter netted yet another triple in the Pilgrims' 4-0 Home Park trouncing of Coventry City. Winger Peter Anderson opened the scoring in the Third Division (South) fixture, but the rest of the game belonged to Carter, who holds the Pilgrims' record for total number of hat-tricks scored by an Argyle player with eight. This one came just seven days after his previous triple, in the FA Cup, and is the only instance of an Argyle player scoring hat-tricks in consecutive games.

SATURDAY 14th DECEMBER 1974

Argyle knocked Crystal Palace – and former manager Malcolm Allison – out of the FA Cup with a dramatic 2-1 second-round victory at Home Park. The Pilgrims had to come back from a goal down against their fellow Third Division side but overcame Dave Swindlehurst's opener through defender Mike Green's 71st-minute chip and striker Bill Rafferty's shot five minutes later. Home Park's schadenfreude of Allison was completed in the second minute of injury-time when goalkeeper Jim Furnell saved Terry Venables' penalty.

TUESDAY 15th DECEMBER 1959

Gary Ball, a Cornish apprentice, was born in St Austell. If there has been a shorter Argyle career than that of Ball's, it will have been over in the blink of an eye. Ball made one sub appearance for the Greens, in a 3-1 Third Division defeat by Sheffield Wednesday in 1979.

SATURDAY 15th DECEMBER 2001

A single goal from French midfielder David Friio secured a 1-0 Third Division victory over Darlington and established a club-record of 19 consecutive league games without defeat. The run had begun on August 27 when, having failed to win any of their opening three matches, the Pilgrims came from behind to win 3-2 at Rushden & Diamonds with goals from Michael Evans, Graham Coughlan, and Brian McGlinchey.

SATURDAY 16th DECEMBER 1950

Argyle's Third Division (South) game at Leyton Orient was abandoned at half-time, with the Pilgrims leading 3-2, after the referee decided the frost-bound surface was a danger to the players. "A mixture of pantomime and ice-ballet" was the succinct and contemporaneous newspaper report of the 45 minutes. Argyle won the re-staged match 2-1 in April.

SUNDAY 16th DECEMBER 1973

Simon Collins, who made 87 appearances for the Pilgrims between 1997 and 1999, was born in Pontefract. Collins started his career as a trainee at Huddersfield Town but did not establish himself with the Terriers and was snapped up by Mick Jones for the Pilgrims.

SATURDAY 17TH DECEMBER 1960

Argyle recorded their heaviest Football League defeat when they were crushed 9-0 at Stoke City in a Second Division game. Stoke had boasted the worst scoring record in the division before the game with just 18 goals. Johnny King potted a hat-trick, the first of which came after just 30 seconds. No-one offered any excuses for the capitulation, although George Kirby and Bill Wright were missing, while goalkeeper Geoff Barnsley played despite two black eyes and a swollen nose.

FRIDAY 17TH DECEMBER 1993

Steve Castle scored the quickest hat-trick in Argyle's history to give Peter Shilton's team of many talents a Second Division victory away at Stockport County. Popular midfielder Castle's triple in the 3-2 win rang in at a mercurial six minutes. Castle, a £225,000 capture from Leyton Orient, finished as the season's leading goalscorer for the Pilgrims, with 21 goals, a figure which no Argyle player managed to top in the subsequent 14 seasons.

SATURDAY 17TH DECEMBER 1994

Forget the festive turkeys, it was Argyle who were stuffed, 7-0 in their Second Division visit to Brentford a week or so before Christmas. The humiliation of Peter Shilton's side completed a stunning 12-1 aggregate for the Bees, who had won 5-1 at Home Park on the opening day of the season. "Things can only get better," was Shilton's lame post-match offering to the Press. They did not. Alarmingly, the Pilgrims lost their second home league game of the campaign 5-1 to Bradford City.

SATURDAY 17TH DECEMBER 2005

There must be something about December 17 and fast scoring. Twelve seasons after Steve Castle's triple-quick hat-trick, Nick Chadwick scored the quickest ever goal by a Pilgrim when he netted in the home Championship game against Crystal Palace after just 11.84 seconds. Argyle went on to win 2-0, but had to wait until the third minute of injury-time for their second strike from Tony Capaldi – surely the longest time ever between the first and second goals in a game.

WEDNESDAY 18TH DECEMBER 1929

Jack Vidler knocked Watford out of the FA Cup when he scored all three goals in a 3-1 second round replay at Home Park. The teams had drawn 1-1 at Vicarage Road the previous Saturday, when Harry Bland had earned the Pilgrims a second chance.

SATURDAY 18TH DECEMBER 1937

Full-back George Silk made his Argyle debut in a 4-0 Second Division defeat at Coventry City. Silk played 90 times for the Pilgrims but it would have been more like 290 had it not been for World War II. He made ten Argyle appearances before the league programme was suspended and was still around after the cessation of hostilities to resume his Plymouth career. He scored once, against West Ham United in 1949, when a hoofed clearance from the touchline inside his own half caught Hammers' goalkeeper Ernie Gregory by surprise.

MONDAY 19TH DECEMBER 1960

Argyle's League Cup fourth round replay against eventual winners Aston Villa caused a bit of head-scratching. The first game had ended 3-3, and when the second reached 90 minutes with the score 0-0 but a waterlogged pitch meant that extra-time, as provided for in the laws of the new competition, was not possible: the question was whether the game should be deemed a draw, in which case a second replay would be required at a neutral venue, or an abandonment. The Football League Management Committee decreed the third match should take place at Home Park. Which it did, but it wasn't played until the following February.

WEDNESDAY 19TH DECEMBER 1973

The Pilgrims continued their progress to the semi-finals of the League Cup with a 2-1 victory at Birmingham City, completing a triple of away wins at top-flight opponents. In a fifth round match played on a Wednesday afternoon because of the power crisis, Third Division Argyle went a goal down but Alan Welsh equalised in the 35th minute. Two minutes later, Steve Davey scored the winner, latching on to goalkeeper Jim Furnell's kick and rubbing the Blues' noses in it with a 30-yard shot.

SATURDAY 20TH DECEMBER 1947

Argyle gained revenge for an opening day 6-1 thrashing by Newcastle United when they trounced the Magpies 3-0 in a Second Division game at Home Park. The eventually-promoted visitors included Len Shackleton, Jackie Milburn and Joe Harvey, but Argyle, who had 42-year-old John Oakes in their defence, won with goals from Frank Squires, Dave Thomas, and George Dews.

SUNDAY 20TH DECEMBER 1987

Goals from Steve Cooper and Mark Smith gave Argyle a 2-1 Second Division victory in the first Football League game at Home Park to be played on a Sunday. A crowd of 11,350 forsook their roast dinners for the tasty win.

SATURDAY 21ST DECEMBER 1929

Tommy Grozier scored four goals as Argyle shattered Crystal Palace with a 6-1 Third Division (South) victory at Home Park. Despite this feat, Scottish right-winger Grozier was not a prolific scorer, although his total of 59 goals in 223 games is a tidy tally.

SATURDAY 21ST DECEMBER 1985

Argyle lost their top-of-the-table Third Division clash with Reading 4-3, having been 3-0 up. Indeed, the Pilgrims led 3-1 with just 11 minutes to play at Elm Park and then conceded three goals in four minutes to the eventual league winners. Kevin Hodges, Steve Cooper and John Clayton scored, before a Dean Horrix penalty and two goals from Trevor Senior hauled Reading level. With time running out, the right royal comeback was completed by Kevin Bremner – who had spent five games on loan at Home Park two years previously – in the 83rd minute.

SATURDAY 22ND DECEMBER 1951

Argyle continued their march to the Third Division (South) title with a comprehensive 5-2 victory over Walsall, with Maurice Tadman scoring a hat-trick. Tadman's 27 goals were at the forefront of the successful season although each one was 'celebrated' in the same understated manner: a brief handshake from a colleague or two, then on with the game.

SATURDAY 22ND DECEMBER 2001

A bad day in a good season, as two club records fell as Argyle were flattened by the Iron. Plymouth's 2-1 Third Division defeat at Scunthorpe United – with both goals coming from former Pilgrim loan player Lee Hodges (not to be confused, as he often was, with Pilgrim Lee Leslie Hodges) – signalled the end of a 19-match undefeated run, a post-World War II record, and single-season best. It also halted their all-time record 12-game unbeaten streak away from home.

FRIDAY 22ND DECEMBER 2006

Argyle completed the purchase of Home Park in a £2.7m deal with Plymouth City Council. The local authority had previously leased the ground to the club under a rental agreement. "For the first time since there's been an Argyle team playing at Home Park, we can truly say it is now our ground," confirmed a jubilant Pilgrims' chairman Paul Stapleton.

SATURDAY 23RD DECEMBER 1922

Rollo Jack, the second and less-famous son of Pilgrims manager Bob Jack, made his Pilgrims' debut in a 1-0 Third Division (South) win at Home Park against Watford. Rollo scored four goals in 15 games before he was whisked away to join brother David at Bolton Wanderers. After failing to hit the same heights as his sibling, he returned to Home Park in 1935 and was working as caretaker-manager following Jack Tresadern's call-up to the Army when the Second World War broke out.

SATURDAY 23RD DECEMBER 1972

Ernie Machin – one of the two central midfielders voted into Argyle's Team of the Century – made his debut for the Pilgrims in a 3-2 Third Division defeat at Watford. He played just 57 times for the Greens in a season and a half with Argyle, but was voted the club's Player of the Year at the end of his only full campaign. That summer he left to join Brighton & Hove Albion. He had arrived at Home Park from Coventry City, where he was the first English football player to successfully challenge an FA fine and suspension in the law courts.

SATURDAY 24TH DECEMBER 1949

'Jumbo' Jack Chisholm made his debut in a 2-1 Second Division match with Chesterfield at Home Park following his record £14,000 move from Sheffield United. The defender had to leave the field for stitches to a head wound but returned, bandaged, to inspire his new side to victory with goals from Maurice Tadman and Frank Squires. He went on to play another 186 games for the Pilgrims and achieved cult status for his larger-than-life personality.

SUNDAY 24TH DECEMBER 1972

Full-back Marc Edworthy, Argyle's Player of the Year in the 1994-95 season, was born in Barnstaple. 'Eddy' worked his way through the Argyle ranks before making his debut as an 18-year-old in a 3-2 home Second Division win against Millwall in 1991. It was the first of four seasons at Home Park, which culminated with the Pilgrims' relegation, his award, and a move to Crystal Palace. Spells at Coventry City, Wolverhampton Wanderers, Norwich City and Derby County followed in a 300-plus game career, as he twice won promotion to the Premiership and played many times in the top-flight.

THURSDAY 25TH DECEMBER 1924

Walter Price made his Argyle debut in a home Third Division (South) 1-1 draw against Devon rivals Exeter City, the only time in Pilgrims' history that a player has been handed a first appearance on Christmas Day – and with the Christmas Day fixture abolished in the 1950s, it's unlikely there will ever be another.

WEDNESDAY 25TH DECEMBER 1929

Argyle tumbled to their first defeat of the Third Division (South) season, 1-0 at Coventry City, in their 18th match of the campaign. Adding the four undefeated games at the end of the previous season, the 22-game sequence without losing set a club record which still stood nearly 80 years later.

TUESDAY 25TH DECEMBER 1951

Argyle drew 2-2 with Bristol City on their way to the Third Division (South) title in the last Christmas Day game to be played at Home Park. Tall Scottish striker Peter Rattray scored both Pilgrims' goals.

SATURDAY 25th DECEMBER 1971

Canadian international striker Giancarlo Michele Corazzin – better known as 'Carlo' – was born in Vancouver. Corazzin scored 23 goals in 85 games for the Pilgrims after joining from Cambridge United in the spring of 1996 to bolster Neil Warnock's Third Division promotion bid. He scored on his debut, but it was two seasons later Corazzin really made his mark, when he finished the season as the club's leading scorer, with 16 goals – an effort which was earned him a share of the fans' Player of the Year award, but it was not enough to save the Pilgrims from relegation back to the basement. Other past Pilgrims who were born on Christmas Day are Bernard Barnes, in 1937, Glen Crowe (1977), and Trevor Shepherd (1946).

SATURDAY 26th DECEMBER 1931

A hat-trick by Jack Vidler helped give Argyle a 5-1 home Second Division victory over Bury. The former soldier's triple was backed up by goals from Ray Bowden and Jack Demmelweek, a fellow serviceman. In fact, Royal Navy product Demmelweek returned to his former employers during the Second World War and took part in Operation Chariot – the 1942 ramming by commandos of the main gate in the German-occupied French port of St Nazaire so that the Tirpitz could not dock anywhere – but was captured and kept prisoner for the rest of the conflict.

FRIDAY 26th DECEMBER 1969

Mike Bickle became only the second Argyle player to score four goals in one game on two separate occasions – Maurice Tadman is the other. Bickle netted his four-goal haul as the Pilgrims showed scant seasonal neighbourliness to Devon rivals Torquay United as they inflicted a 6-0 Third Division defeat on them. It was the Gulls' first loss in 11 league games.

WEDNESDAY 26th DECEMBER 1984

Tommy Tynan scored a hat-trick for the Pilgrims in their Christmas derby with Bristol City at Ashton Gate but it was not enough to prevent Argyle suffering a 4-3 Third Division defeat. Tynan is the only Argyle player to have come off the field a loser after scoring a hat-trick for Argyle.

FRIDAY 26TH DECEMBER 2003

Pilgrims followers who made the trip along the south coast were singing in the rain, as Second Division champions-in-waiting Argyle won 2-0 at AFC Bournemouth, amidst a rain-lashed gale. The first of the two goals was one of those trademark strikes from captain Paul Wotton. His 40-yard stunner was also the Pilgrims' 5000th goal. David Norris hit a wind-assisted second as Argyle adapted to the elements much better than their hosts.

SATURDAY 27TH DECEMBER 1924

A hat-trick from Sammy Black, the first of his record-breaking Argyle career, helped the Pilgrims to a 5-0 home Third Division (South) victory over Norwich City. Bert Batten and Percy Cherrett scored the Pilgrims' other goals. Scot Black, who was signed from Kirkintilloch Rob Roy, is second in the all-time Argyle appearances list, with 491 games, and top Pilgrims' scorer, with 185 goals.

SATURDAY 27TH DECEMBER 1930

Argyle recorded one of their heaviest ever Football League defeats when they lost 9-1 at Everton. There were mitigating circumstances: the Pilgrims trotted out at Goodison less than 24 hours after beating Cardiff City 5-1 at Home Park, followed by a ten-hour all-night train journey that arrived on Merseyside at 6am. The hosts had been without a Second Division game of their own game the previous day. In driving rain, and on a pitch so bad that the referee held the pre-match coin-toss on the sidelines, the Pilgrims were a goal down to Bill Dean within a minute. Dean scored three more, and his four-goal haul was matched by Jimmy Stein.

TUESDAY 27TH DECEMBER 1960

Wilf Carter became the only Argyle player to ever score five goals in a Football League game when the Pilgrims beat Charlton Athletic 6-4 in a Second Division game at Home Park. The former West Brom man raced to a hat-trick within 33 minutes and added a fourth before the interval. It was not until his fifth, from a penalty, which made the score 5-4, that Argyle finally shook off Charlton, and Alex Jackson finished the scoring to make the result a mirror-image of the result between the two sides at the Valley 24 hours earlier.

MONDAY 28TH DECEMBER 1925

Paddy Blatchford, a winger from Saltash, was born. Blatchford gave up a career in the Admiralty for Argyle but was stymied by Alex Govan's domination of his position. His high-water mark in three seasons from 1948 came in a friendly against Southampton, when he repeatedly skinned opposition full-back Alf Ramsey.

WEDNESDAY 28TH DECEMBER 2005

Argyle borrowed industrial blowers from Plymouth City Airport in an attempt to thaw out Home Park but the ambitious bid to play a Championship match against Preston North End was thwarted when temperatures fell. The late postponement infuriated Preston manager Billy Davies, and he was not overly pleased when his side only got a point from a 0-0 draw when the game was eventually staged.

SATURDAY 29TH DECEMBER 1923

Harry Raymond made the last of his 67 Football League appearances for Argyle in a 1-1 Division Three (South) game against Merthyr at Home Park. Raymond was the first Argyle player to win international honours, playing three times for the England amateur side, and served the Pilgrims for 16 years. For this, he was awarded a testimonial against the famous amateurs, Corinthian Casuals.

SATURDAY 29TH DECEMBER 1951

George Dews and Peter Rattray each scored twice as Argyle beat Shrewsbury Town 6-1 at Home Park to add momentum to their Third Division (South) title challenge. Maurice Tadman and Alex Govan were also on target in a win which sparked eight successive victories.

SATURDAY 30TH DECEMBER 1950

Billy Rafferty, one half of the striking partnership of the dream 1974/75 season, was born in Port Glasgow. He joined Argyle from Blackpool in March 1974 and left for Carlisle United two years later, having scored 35 league goals in 90 matches. Although Paul Mariner went on to gain the greater fame and rewards, there were many – including Mariner himself – who felt Rafferty was the better player. Certainly, Rafferty outscored Mariner, by 23 goals to 20, for Tony Waiters' 1975 Third Division promotion winners.

SATURDAY 30TH DECEMBER 1978

Stoke City's Lee Chapman made the final appearance of his four-game loan spell with Argyle when he came on as a substitute in a 2-0 Third Division defeat by Gillingham. The future England B international, who forged a career with some of the country's top clubs, made his league debut with the Pilgrims in a 1-1 home draw against Watford three weeks earlier.

SATURDAY 31ST DECEMBER 1921

Frank Richardson's amazing debut season for Argyle continued with the second of three hat-tricks in a 3-1 home Third Division (South) victory over Swansea Town. With a total of 41 goals in 67 games, he was much in demand but failed to reproduce his Argyle form in subsequent stints with Stoke City, West Ham United, Swindon Town and Reading.

SATURDAY 31ST DECEMBER 1955

Bob Swiggs made his Argyle debut in a 1-1 Second Division draw against Hull City at Home Park. Swiggs, a prolific goalscorer in non-league circles with St Blazey, went on to play just two more times for the Greens, but was halfway to making history. The other half came 29 years later, when son Bradley became the first son of a former player to wear the green since the days of Bob Jack and his offspring. Sadly for Bradley, he made one fewer appearance than dad before also becoming a hit in local football.